THE NO-TITLE COOKBOOK

A Label Free Approach to Whole Food Cooking

DREW MULVEY MS, CDN

HybridGlobal
PUBLISHING

Published by
Hybrid Global Publishing
301 E. 57th Street, 4th floor
New York, NY 10022

Manufactured in the United States of America,
or in the United Kingdom when distributed elsewhere.

Mulvey, Drew
The No-Title Cookbook:
A Label-Free Approach to Whole Food Cooking
ISBN: 978-1-951943-14-1
eBook: 978-1-951943-15-8
LCCN: 2020907508

Cover design by: Natasha Clawson
Copyediting by: Gary M. Krebs
Interior design: Medlar Publishing Solutions Pvt Ltd., India

www.notitlecookbook.com

DISCLAIMER:

*The author of this book does not dispense medical advice and does not prescribe the use of
any of the techniques or recipes in this book as a form of treatment for physical, mental,
or emotional problems without the advice of a trained health professional. The information
and recipes contained herein should be considered as only one reference in your quest to
lead a healthier dietary life. Every person's situation and needs are different. The author
and publisher assume no responsibility for your actions and advise consultation with
your health care practitioner prior to embarking on any diet or nutritional plan.*

The thief's purpose is to steal and kill and destroy.
My purpose is to give them a rich and satisfying life.
—**Jesus,** John 10:10, The Bible NLT

ACKNOWLEDGEMENTS

I would like to give special thanks to the two people who helped get this book published: Gary M. Krebs and Karen Strauss. I would also like to thank all of my friends and Instagram followers who continuously support me with their encouraging words and are always pushing me to be the best version of myself. I couldn't have done it without you. Most importantly, I would like to thank my family—especially my mother, who walked with me through the good and bad of my journey and became the inspiration for this book after having overcome cancer.

TABLE OF CONTENTS

THE MOTIVATION BEHIND THE BOOK

I would say that my health journey started from the womb. Wait—don't all of our health journeys start from the womb?

Let's press the fast-forward button. I was a fourteen-year-old eighth grader. I was overweight, depleted of energy, eating a processed food diet (also known as the Standard American Diet) and diagnosed with insomnia, Irritable Bowel Syndrome (IBS), depression, and anxiety. While suffering from all of these maladies, I was also a competitive diver at the beginning of her career. With all of these factors impacting my athletic performance and taking a toll on my quality of life, I knew I needed a change.

Since I loved animals and wanted to lose weight, it was only natural that I became introduced to a vegetarian diet—the first of my exploratory nutrition journeys. I maintained vegetarianism throughout high school and into about four months of college, but then had to make some changes. Apparently, the combination of being a competitive diver and a stressed-out college student with low ferritin levels (a blood protein containing iron) and a diminishing immune system resulted in having to forfeit my vegetarian diet and eat red meat every other day.

Was it an ego downer? Yes, slightly. Then I had an epiphany: I had been a vegetarian more for "the culture" than caring about its actual health benefits and learning how to do it right.

When I entered my twenties I battled even more health issues: fibromyalgia, *Candidiasis* (aka *Candida*), chronic fatigue syndrome, and immune dysfunction. The *Candida* became particularly troubling. Without getting too technical, the ailment is caused by a build-up of the fungus *Candida albicans*, which leads to an overgrowth that can affect the digestive tract. In my case, it spread throughout my entire body and attacked my white blood cells. The symptoms resemble that of HIV (although it's not the same disease).

My situation left me no choice except to try something different, and my first medicinal therapeutic nutrition lesson emerged: an "anti-*Candida*" diet. I began to explore how food and nutrition may be used to combat infirmities. I lost a lot of weight and, for the first time in my life, started to feel like I had energy.

For the next several years I experimented with different diets and alternative recipes. At one point I considered myself paleo (a diet consisting of foods that could be obtained by hunting and gathering); at another, I mostly identified with vegan. I found out that I have food sensitivities to gluten, dairy, eggs, quinoa, and nightshades. I have dealt with bacterial overgrowth while implementing a low FODMAP diet (an acronym for Fermentable Oligosaccharides, Disaccharides, Monosaccharides, and Polyols, meaning short chain carbohydrates and sugar alcohols that are poorly absorbed by the body, typically resulting in abdominal pain and bloating); been on a vegan Daniel Fast (a twenty-one-day diet plan intended to mimic the eating habits of the titular Biblical character); and incorporated TCM (Traditional Chinese Medicine) principles using food energetics (five branches of nutrition based on thermal properties) to target specific ailments.

In other words, you name the diet and I've probably tried it. My diet experimentations were accompanied by extensive recipe research. I have experienced firsthand the difficulties in finding options for maintaining my diet along with stimulating the palette. I have always been a foodie with particular tastes and know how certain temptations can throw me off track. Through this process I learned that *yes*—I, too, am a human! Imagine that.

By following alternative recipes and learning how to swap ingredients, I acquired great foundational knowledge to get my creative juices flowing—no matter what dietary journey I happened to be on.

Did this mean that I had to be on a specific diet forever? Did this also require my having to identify with a specific diet? *Au contraire.* Through this adventure, I learned another important lesson: the value of listening to your body and incorporating a whole food, label-free diet. I realized that my dietary preferences did not obligate me to choose titles for them. Food can be used as a journey to a personal discovery of one's unique identity. Might I say, this is a very freeing place to be. Food can quite therapeutic, even when it's not being characterized—which is how I arrived at the title of this book: *The No-Title Cookbook*. Within the pages that follow, I will share with you my most successful culinary adventures, most of which involve the elimination of gluten and dairy—both of which tend to be common problem areas for people with health issues ranging from IBS and celiac to heart disease and lactose intolerance.

Another reason why I'm so passionate about food stems from its use as medicine. As you will discover in an upcoming section entitled "Functional Foods," certain items we eat contain specific compounds with properties that promote additional health benefits.

A good portion of the recipes in this book were not only a culmination of my alternative culinary adventures but were inspired by a recent event in my life. In March 2018, my mother was diagnosed with follicular lymphoma (a type of cancer that affects white blood cells) and endured chemotherapy to get rid of it. Through her treatment and by incorporating many of these recipes, changing her diet, and activating her faith, she has been in remission since August 2018.

Below is the picture of us celebrating her victory over cancer. Now I am on a mission to help others live a life of abundance by satisfying the palate while helping to potentially prevent cancer and other chronic diseases. It is with great pleasure that I share my passion from the kitchen and present to you some fully functional and nutrient-dense recipes to add to any lifestyle—title-free, of course.

THERAPEUTIC DIETS

There are numerous diets that address how to bypass specific foods, whether causes are due to food sensitivities, weight loss, or health concerns. Below are just a few that I will be covering in this cookbook.

GLUTEN-FREE

Description: Gluten is a protein that can be found in grains such as rye, barley, wheat, kamut, farro, and some oats. For some individuals, it may cause problems in their bodies due to the protein's ability to escape from the intestinal wall if permeation is present. In celiac disease, the tight junctions in the epithelium holding the intestine together do not function properly and thus proteins known as anti-gliadin antibodies escape, causing symptoms ranging from headaches and rashes to common gastrointestinal issues, such as diarrhea, bloating, and cramping.

Many people have chosen to adopt this diet, as grains containing gluten have been deemed as being "pro-inflammatory." Even in the sports world, a Gluten-Free diet has been prescribed to increase performance, particularly among endurance athletes.

Some individuals suffer from Non-Celiac Gluten Sensitivity. For these individuals, elimination and therapeutic diets have been introduced in order to address their sensitivities. This approach has also been used for autoimmune conditions as well.

Guide: Gluten-Free recipes are designated with a *GF*.

PALEO

Description: The reasoning behind this diet—which is also known as the "Hunter-Gatherer Diet"—is the concept that consuming the foods eaten by our Paleolithic ancestors will be better accepted and processed by our bodies today. This diet emphasizes consumption of more fruits and vegetables, nuts and seeds, and oils (such as olive oil and coconut oil) and incorporation of quality animal products, such as grass-fed beef, organic chicken, wild caught fish, and pasture-raised eggs. Grains, beans, and dairy are eliminated from the diet, as they were not available for consumption before the agricultural revolution and are considered to be "pro-inflammatory."

Guide: Recipes that are paleo are designated with a *P*.

VEGAN/VEGETARIAN

Description: Vegetarian diets, also known as lacto-ovo, emphasize a greater consumption of plant-based foods but with the inclusion of dairy and sometimes eggs. When all animal products are excluded, it becomes better known as Vegan. Since these individuals are not eating meat, the protein sources include beans/legumes, nuts and seeds, and grains.

A protein consists of an assortment of twenty amino acids. Out of these, thirteen can be made by the body from other amino acids and nine are essential, meaning they have to be obtained from the diet. For a food to be considered a *complete* protein, all nine essential amino acids must be present in it or in combination with something else in a dish. Plants are often *incomplete* proteins, which means they do not possess all of these essential amino acids. Only soy and quinoa contain all nine. Foods with incomplete proteins are often paired together as *complimentary* proteins. These consist of pairing food groups such as legumes with grains, nuts with legumes, or nuts with grains, in dishes to fill in the missing amino acids.

The perfect example of a complementary protein would be traditional rice and beans and, of course, tacos. Who knew there was nutritional reasoning behind this, as well as being a delicious addition to a plant-based meal?

The scientific explanation behind this stems from the notion that the high fiber content in the foods contribute to a decrease in bulk transit time, which can act as a preventative measure against colon problems later on. The individual also reaps additional nutritional benefits from the wide array of antioxidants that these plants deliver and may also help to lower LDL cholesterol, triglycerides, and promote insulin sensitivity.

Guide: Vegetarian and Vegan dishes are designated with a *V*.

ELIMINATION/
ANTI-INFLAMMATORY DIET

Description: Food sensitivities—which may cause various physical symptoms, including headaches and bloating, as well as minor manifestations, such as a runny nose, lethargy, or brain fog—are more common than we think. Over time, even minute, unrecognized sensitivities may contribute to low-grade inflammation that have been the root of several chronic diseases, especially autoimmune-related. This particular diet eliminates the most common food allergens and potential inflammatory foods, including: gluten, dairy, soy, corn, citrus, tree nuts, nightshade vegetables (tomatoes, eggplants, peppers, potatoes, paprika, and goji berries), peanuts and, for some people, chocolate and eggs.

The theory behind this diet is that abstaining from these foods may help alleviate symptoms often caused by increased inflammation. Those who might benefit from this diet are individuals suffering from autoimmune conditions, such as lupus, rheumatoid arthritis, and IBD (inflammatory bowel disease), to name a few.

Guide: Anti-inflammatory dishes are designated with an *AI*.

To summarize the Guides in the above, each recipe contains the following acronym:

GF = Gluten-Free
V = Vegan
P = Paleo
AI = Anti-inflammatory

Additionally, for those who are lactose intolerant or have allergies to dairy products, we have one more acronym:

DF = Dairy-Free

GLUTEN-FREE GRAINS

Gluten has perhaps received an undeserved bad rap, but the truth is that is has become something of an issue for many people. If a person does have a gluten problem, one of the most difficult things to do is figure out what can replace this diet staple. Below you will find descriptions of several gluten-free grains, along with their functional properties. Many of the recipes in this book are free of this protein and provide healthy alternatives.

MILLET

This is one of my absolute favorite grains. Millet has a slight nutty flavor and properties that help the body with digestion, as well as fight diabetes, produce energy (due to its alkalinity), and act like a diuretic. It can be used as a delicious substitute for grits, oats, and rice in stir fries.

If you are feeling a little hot, consider adding millet to foods in order to help "cool off."

According to traditional Chinese medicine, it may have a cooling effect in the body.

BUCKWHEAT

Buckwheat also has something of a nutty flavor and is a little grittier than the other substitutes. Though placed under the grain category buckwheat, or groats, it is actually not a wheat and is therefore gluten-free. Buckwheat is high in magnesium and may help to stimulate appetite and promote better blood circulation. It is also a great source of the antioxidant rutin, a bioflavonoid that may help strengthen blood vessels, improve integrity of the capillaries, regulate blood pressure, and even help fight cancer.

BROWN RICE

This is probably one of the easiest grains to incorporate into a diet, as it has been a long-time staple of many cultural dishes, including curries, rice and beans, and taco bowls. Brown rice is a whole-grain rice in which the outer inedible portion (known as the hull) is removed (as with white rice), but the nutrition-rich bran layer and cereal germ remain (unlike in white rice). This increases its fiber and B vitamin content and makes it slower to digest without spiking insulin levels. Brown rice has become such a staple in gluten-free diets that there are now many pastas, breads, and baked goods containing this ingredient that you can purchase in grocery and specialty stores and incorporate into a variety of recipes.

According to Eastern Medicine, brown rice is warming in thermal nature and therefore recommended in cases of "coldness" and "dampness," which can contribute to digestive upset, decreased vitality, and possible brain fog. It is also considered a hypoallergenic grain, which means it is suitable for most of the population. What better way to warm your body than with some curry served over this delightful gluten-free grain?

QUINOA

Contrary to popular belief, quinoa is actually a seed and not a grain. Compared to other seeds and grains, it has the highest protein content. Quinoa is also an excellent source of energy-boosting B vitamins, calming magnesium, and plant-based calcium, which makes it a suitable alternative for those who have a dairy/lactose allergy or are vegan. Practitioners of Chinese Medicine consider it to be warming in nature and may benefit individuals who experience coldness in their bodies.

OATS (MARKED GLUTEN-FREE)

There is a lot of scientific debate surrounding gluten found in oats. Some sources believe that they contain their own sort of gluten; others believe this is a result of contaminated equipment. Here is my take: When in doubt, oats not specifically labeled "gluten-free" are out.

Some of the health benefits of gluten-free oats may include: cancer prevention; lowered cholesterol; stable blood sugar; alleviated indigestion; renewal of bones and connective tissue; and improved reproductive function. It is truly a versatile grain that may be served as part of a nutritious breakfast, while the flour can incorporated into multiple gluten-free baked goods and vegan delicacies.

AMARANTH

Though it is often labeled a "grain," amaranth is actually a seed. (Are you starting to notice a trend?) Amaranth has a slightly bitter taste and is an excellent source of plant protein, which makes the muscle-building macronutrient a staple in many vegan diets. Very close in composition to quinoa, amaranth is another excellent source of plant-based calcium and ideal for people with an aversion to dairy and those whose diets are 100% plant-based. It is often used in breakfast dishes as a porridge.

SORGHUM

Sorghum is a grain that is often used as an alternative to couscous in dishes. It is an excellent source of fiber (packing about eight grams per ¼ cup dry), magnesium, zinc, and selenium, which is beneficial for insulin sensitivity, easing nerves, increasing immunity, and improving the digestion of protein. Sorghum is widely used in the West Indies as a flour and used to prepare flat tortilla-like breads called Chapatis. I enjoy it in the morning as a substitute for usual oats.

FUNCTIONAL FOODS

Functional foods contain nutrients with benefits for physiological function beyond that of basic nutrition. The ancient Greeks valued specific foods for their therapeutic properties. Hippocrates, an ancient Greek physician, went as far as coining the phrase "Let food be thy medicine and medicine be thy food." There are numerous functional foods that are highly valued in countries around the world today, but I would like to highlight just a few of my favorites, which appear throughout this cookbook. Please note that I would include buckwheat, millet, and oats in this section, but they are included in the previous section under Gluten-Free Grains.

ACAI BERRIES

Acai berries are chock full of antioxidants with free radical scavenging properties that may act as possible preventatives against chronic diseases. They can also help improve digestion and repair the breakdown of body tissue from mechanical stress caused by exercise. With their high antioxidant levels, this may be beneficial to combat inflammation prone conditions, such as insulin resistance and heart disease.

ADUKI BEANS

These beans are widely used in traditional Chinese Medicine due to their many healing properties involving body humidity or "dampness." Dampness is believed to be at the root of inflammation and the cause of many chronic diseases we see today. These little beans internally dry those damp conditions, which can be caused by a stressful lifestyle or ingestion of too much sugar, fat, salt, and processed foods. Aduki beans are warming in nature, may help with blood stagnation, reduce swelling, and even promote weight loss. They are an excellent dietary staple under times of heightened stress, as they tonify the adrenals and kidneys.

AVOCADOS

These tropical fruits are powerhouses when it comes to nutrients. They contain more potassium than bananas, are rich in fiber and monounsaturated fats, and are a source of lecithin, which helps with proper brain function! If that's not enough, avocados also rank high among the list of copper-rich foods. Copper, a mineral, is invaluable for bone production, immune system function, and red blood cell formation.

BEETS

Beets are touted as one of the best blood tonics and liver healthy foods. Their high antioxidant and phytonutrient content have demonstrated an incredible capacity to aid in muscle recovery post-workout among professional and amateur athletes. Beets are also a natural source of arginine—an amino acid responsible for stimulating the production of nitric oxide, which provides a testosterone boost for men and also aids in muscle recovery, growth, and the delivery of vital nutrients. They are beneficial for women's reproductive health as well, as they promote menses and can assist hormone regulation when ingested with carrots.

CARROTS

This is an easy vegetable to add to any dish in the form of soups, roasted veggies, or baked goods. Carrots are high in antioxidant and cancer-fighting beta carotene. They are also beneficial for bones and connective tissue, due to their silicon content. Another fun fact: They help digestion and can alleviate heartburn and excess stomach acid. Some health practitioners believe that carrots may improve liver function and even act as an antiparasitic to help push pinworms and roundworms out of the intestines.

CELERY

These lovely green stalks are much more than just a base for your soups. Celery may be beneficial for colon health and weight loss, as it is high in fiber and water. It is also an excellent source of vitamin K, which helps with blood clotting as well as bone health. Celery contains a large amount of silicon, which is a component of the bones and also beneficial for healthy arteries and joints. Many people drink celery juice in the morning to improve digestion.

CHIA SEEDS

I love the nutrient-rich value of chia seeds. Chia is an excellent source of fiber and one of the highest sources of plant-based omega-3 fatty acids. Its high mucilaginous (meaning it becomes gooey and soluble when mixed with water) content enables it to help ease constipation and keep the colon healthy. On the downside, chia does contain a significant amount of phytic acid (phytates), a compound that inhibits the absorption of iron, calcium, and zinc. The best way to consume chia seeds are when they are soaked.

CINNAMON

Cinnamon is warming in nature, which makes it ideal for fall and winter dishes that are often prepared when the weather starts to cool down. Not only does it add a little spice to apples and pies, it helps with production of digestive enzymes from the pancreas. Cinnamon is also antibacterial and contains potent antioxidants that have been used to help fight cancer and as a functional food to promote insulin sensitivity (allowing the body's cells to use blood glucose more effectively and reduce blood sugar).

COCONUT

This tropical delicacy is both delicious and nutritious! Coconut is a rich source of medium chain triglycerides, which are noted for their ability to help decrease a person's body weight due to the increased efficiency of the body while the food is being ingested. It also contains magnesium, a chemical element that is beneficial for bone health, heart health, and insulin sensitivity. Lauric acid, which may help treat skin ailments, such as psoriasis and acne, comprise about half of the fatty acids found in coconut oil. Coconut also has anti-parasitic properties that fight off intestinal worms. Interesting fact: Though coconuts are a tropical fruit, they are warming in nature helping to build the qi (the body's vitality and life force).

CRANBERRIES

These little berries are more than just a holiday condiment spread over roasted turkey during the holidays. They are one of the lowest sugar fruits, which makes them an ideal staple for those with blood sugar issues as well as people adhering to a low carbohydrate diet. They are an excellent source of fiber and rich in vitamin C. Cranberries even contain manganese, which boosts immunity and promotes healthy cartilage and bone development. In addition, cranberries are filled with polyphenols (aka proanthocyanidins), which help improve heart and joint health and fight infections, cancer, and allergies. Current research has found that this component may be an effective antimicrobial agent against *E. coli*—a bacteria responsible for illnesses such as UTIs, gastroenteritis, kidney infections—and *H. pylori* (Helicobacter pylori), a bacteria responsible for ulcers.

DARK CHOCOLATE

Aren't you glad to hear that we don't have to eliminate this amazing food? In fact, I actually encourage it (unless you have an allergy, of course)! Dark chocolate is an excellent source of magnesium, which can help calm down the muscles and the mind. Like cranberries, dark chocolate contains polyphenols, which are beneficial for heart and joint health. It is also a great source of flavanols, compounds that are also good for the heart. Cocoa, one of the main substances in dark chocolate, is actually one of the most advantageous foods for you. Studies have shown that it improves cognition and aids in recovery after a tough workout.

FLAX

Flax, a plant that is cultivated for its seeds, contains lignans (yet another polyphenol, like cranberries and dark chocolate), which help stimulate apoptosis—a process that can help eliminate pre-cancerous cells, especially in the intestines. Flax and flax oil have been used in cancer treatments, such as the Budwig Diet. The fiber found in flax helps with digestive transit time, lowers LDL cholesterol levels, and reduces inflammation. Flax is a natural source of plant-based omega-3s, which are beneficial for the arteries and the heart and help boost immunity.

GINGER

Ginger is a nutrient-rich powerhouse that also happens to make an excellent tea. Some of the compounds in ginger are "anti" to help combat a wide range of health issues: anti-inflammatory, anti-platelet, anti-ulcer, anti-microbial, antiviral, antioxidant, and anti-parasitic. It can aid digestion, stimulating gastric and bile secretion. Ginger root is warming in nature and can be used to enhance circulation to the lower half of the body, such as the legs, colon, ovaries, and reproductive organs. When fresh, ginger can be eaten with high protein foods, such as meat and beans, to help decrease uric acid content—which is usually the cause of gout.

MACA

Maca powder is a wonderful addition to food that couples well with chocolate. Maca cocoa pancakes, please? Maca stands out as a superfood, due to its ability to help with post-workout muscle recovery and also balance hormones. Considered to be an adaptogenic herb, maca helps the immune system by allowing the body to adapt to increased stressors.

PEPPERMINT

This is usually a wonderful addition to chocolate dishes during the holidays. (Peppermint mocha, anyone?) But it is so much more than just a flavorful add in. Peppermint can be beneficial as an antimicrobial (killing bad microorganisms) and help resolve headaches. Peppermint has also been used for Irritable Bowel Syndrome (IBS) and dyspepsia to reduce bloating and digestive issues.

POMEGRANATES

Personally, I love these little seeds and all the compounds they possess that help increase vitality. Pomegranates are beneficial to counter benign prostatic hyperplasia (BPH or prostate enlargement) in men. Eight ounces of pomegranate juice a day are often recommended for this. This ancient fruit has several other healing properties. The juice alone contains branched chain amino acids for muscle repair, sulfur containing antioxidants to help the liver detoxify toxins, and compounds that help improve joint health and increase nitric oxide production in the body, a molecule beneficial for regulating heart rhythm and improving delivery of nutrients to skeletal muscles.

PUMPKINS

I get pumped about this one when autumn comes around. Along with squash, it is a seasonal staple that is warming in nature and excellent for building up qi (energy force or vitality). When the body experiences lethargy, poor digestion, brain fog, and chronic disease, it may mean there is a dampness or humidity in the body. Pumpkin contains properties that may help dry up the body's humidity and fight off conditions such as eczema and dysentery. The fiber and antioxidant content of pumpkins make them ideal for blood sugar regulation. When cooked, pumpkin has anti-parasitic properties that destroy intestinal worms. As if we needed another reason to make pumpkin pie-flavored dishes!

TURMERIC

Turmeric, a bright yellow spice that has been incorporated in dishes and used medicinally in India for thousands of years, boasts myriad health benefits. It contains antiviral, antioxidant, anti-inflammatory, and antimicrobial compounds that make it an excellent addition to any diet to help prevent and possibly eliminate innumerable illnesses, including brain disorders, heart disease, cancer, arthritis, depression, and even flatulence. Not enough for you? Many nutritionists and health care practitioners are now going as far as touting turmeric as an anti-aging supplement as well.

BREAKFAST RECIPES

OMELET

ANTIOXIDANT VEGETABLE OMELET

Makes 1 serving

One of the easiest ways to get your essential servings of veggies and fill your body with nutrition is to create an omelet. Specifically, the Antioxidant Vegetable Omelet was formulated based on its antioxidant and nutrient profiles that help detox carcinogens or target cancer cells. What better way to start the day knowing your body is fighting off free radicals while providing muscle-building protein? The best part is that it's a delicious combination and so easy to put together, as it can be incorporated into any busy schedule.

2 organic, pasture-raised eggs
1 dash of non-dairy milk
Salt and pepper to taste
½ red onion, chopped
2 cups organic spinach
1 bulb garlic, mashed
½ avocado

1 tbsp coconut oil or extra virgin olive oil (divided)

Beat the eggs with non-dairy milk and salt and pepper. Set it aside.

In a separate pan, sauté the spinach, garlic, and onions over medium heat in ½ tbsp coconut oil. Set it aside.

Heat ½ tbsp of oil over low-medium heat. Pour eggs over. Bunch the eggs in the middle of the pan while swirling around the loose egg. Place a cover on the skillet over the eggs for 30 seconds to slightly cook the top.

Once done, pour in the spinach, red onions, garlic, and avocado. Gently fold in the eggs and cook for 30 seconds on one side.

Note: If you do not want the eggs to burn, leave them out until they reach room temperature.

Guide: GF, DF

> **Nutrition Facts (1 serving)**
>
> Calories: 433; Total Fat: 36.3 g; Sat Fat: 16.6 g; Cholesterol: 372 mg; Sodium: 192 mg; Total Carbohydrates: 16 g; Dietary Fiber: 7.5 g; Total Sugars: 3.8 g; Protein: 16.5 g; Vitamin D: 82 mcg; Calcium: 12 mg; Iron: 4 mg; Potassium: 961 mg

PANCAKES AND CREPES

SWEET POTATO CREPES WITH CHOCOLATE OVERNIGHT OATS

Makes 5 (9-inch) crepes

I like to mix up my breakfasts—minus the flour and with a twist. Therefore, I paired two delightful breakfasts together in one dish: crepes and overnight oats. The use of coconut flour in place of real flour adds insoluble fiber to the dish, while the beta carotene in the sweet potato and glycine in the collagen peptides provide a rich source of antioxidants that are beneficial for free radical scavenging.

For the Crepes:

2 ½ oz sweet potato, diced and steamed

2–3 cups filtered water

½ cup unsweetened coconut milk
(from a carton)

½ cup gluten-free flour blend (1 tbsp
coconut flour, 3 tbsps, almond flour,
¼ cup arrowroot flour)

1 organic, pasture-raised egg

3 tbsps water

¼ tsp sea salt

Dash of cinnamon

1 ½ tbsps coconut oil

For the Overnight Oats:

½ cup organic, gluten-free rolled oats

¾ cup unsweetened coconut milk

1 tbsp cocoa powder

2 scoops collagen peptides (optional)

1 tbsp chia seeds

Stevia to taste

For the Oats:

Combine all ingredients for the oats in a mason jar and transfer them to the refrigerator to sit overnight.

For the Crepes:

Dice the sweet potatoes and weigh them out on a food scale.

Place 2–3 cups filtered water in a medium pot.

Add steamer insert to the pot and place diced sweet potatoes in the insert. Cover and place the pot over high flame until steam forms. Turn heat down to low-high flame and continue to cook sweet potatoes until tender, about 5–6 minutes.

Blend all ingredients, aside from the coconut oil, together in a food processor until fully incorporated. Transfer to a bowl, cover, and refrigerate for 2 hours or overnight.

For smaller crepes, use an 8-inch skillet and place over medium heat. Brush coconut oil on the skillet and allow it to melt and come to a sizzle. Once the oil is sizzling, remove the pan from heat and pour ¼ cup of crepe mix on the skillet.

Tilt and swirl the batter over the face of the pan and place back on the heat. Let it cook for about 30–60 seconds. With a thin spatula, flip the crepe and allow it to cook for another 30 seconds.

Transfer the finished crepe to a plate lined with a paper towel and let it cool.

Slather half a crepe with a small amount of overnight oats and nut butter of choice. Fold it into quarters.

Add your favorite toppings or more nut butter!

Note: You will have some oats left over. They can be part of your breakfast for the next day or you can save them for another day of crepes!

Guide: GF, DF

Nutrition Facts (1 serving)

Calories: 307; Total Fat: 22.4 g; Sat Fat: 17.1 g; Cholesterol: 37 mg; Sodium: 215 mg; Total Carbohydrates: 16.8 g; Dietary Fiber: 5.7 g; Total Sugars: 3.2 g; Protein: 13 g; Vitamin D: 4 mcg; Calcium: 62 mg; Iron: 3 mg; Potassium: 323 mg

CARROT CAKE OAT FLOUR PANCAKES

Makes 1–2 servings

Many of the gluten-free pancake recipes contain eggs as one of the ingredients. When I learned that I needed to nix the eggs due to a sensitivity, I conducted some research to find a substitute and stumbled upon a recipe that used oat flour as the base. (I'd like to give a shout out to my instab-uddy @plantbasedpilipina, now @arla.selcedo, for these.) Carrot cake flavors are a staple in my home. Having them as part of a hearty breakfast warms my soul. As always, I tweaked this recipe to cater to my carrot cake craving, and these lovely pancakes were established. Once I discovered oat flour, it became a staple in my pancake recipes.

1 cup organic rolled oats, processed into a flour

10 organic baby carrots, grated

½ cup organic apple sauce

2 tsps apple cider vinegar

2 tsps aluminum-free baking powder

¾ cups water (or non-dairy milk)

1 tsp cinnamon

½ tsp ginger

½ tsp nutmeg

1–2 tbsps organic raisins

1–2 tbsps coconut oil (for cooking)

Dash of stevia

Dash of sea salt

Place the baby carrots in a food processor and process until the carrots are grated. Put aside.

Add the oats to the blender and process until it becomes a powder.

Add all ingredients in a blender aside from the raisins and carrots and puree. Let it sit for about 5 minutes.

In the meantime, place the coconut oil on a skillet over medium heat. Use ¼ cup portions for pouring the pancake mix on the skillet. Cook each side for about 2–3 minutes.

Enjoy with your favorite topping!

Guide: GF, DF, AI, V

Nutrition Facts (1 serving)

Calories: 291; Total Fat: 31.6 g; Sat Fat: 25.8 g; Cholesterol: 0 mg; Sodium: 149 mg; Total Carbohydrates: 49.3 g; Dietary Fiber: 9.5 g; Total Sugars: 11.1 g; Protein: 8.6 g; Vitamin D: 0 mcg; Calcium: 123 mg; Iron: 4 mg; Potassium: 581 mg

Makes 1–2 servings (3–4 pancakes)

For a time, while I was trying to experiment with different flours, I decided that the fad diet for the season was paleo. I wanted something with robust flavor, naturally sweetened, and a great source of fiber to feed the gut bacteria and fuel my day. My search for the right recipes proved fruitless, so I concocted my own—and thus we have Nix the Flour Banana Chocolate Chip Pancakes. The blend of coconut flour and almond flour adds a little density, which I personally like as a characteristic in my pancakes.

2 tbsps coconut flour

1 tbsp almond flour

1 tbsp arrowroot flour

2 organic, pasture-raised eggs

¼ tsp baking soda

¼ tsp vanilla extract

½ banana

½ tbsp mini chocolate chips

⅛–¼ cup unsweetened coconut milk

1–2 tbsps coconut oil (for cooking)

In a small bowl, mix all of the dry ingredients and place aside.

In a larger bowl, mash the banana. Add the rest of the wet ingredients and whisk everything together.

Add the dry ingredients to the wet ingredients while continuing to whisk.

When all the ingredients are well mixed and incorporated, stir in the chocolate chips.

Heat the coconut oil on a skillet over medium heat. With ¼ cup measuring cup, scoop the pancake mix on to the skillet. Cook until the top starts to bubble (for about 3–5 minutes) and then flip.

Transfer to a plate, add some pure maple syrup, and have yourself a taste bud pleasing breakfast.

Guide: GF, DF, P

Nutrition Facts (1 serving)

Calories: 427; Total Fat: 29.1 g; Sat Fat: 19.1 g; Cholesterol: 327 mg; Sodium: 469 mg; Total Carbohydrates: 29.4 g; Dietary Fiber: 7.5 g; Total Sugars: 12.6 g; Protein: 14.6 g; Vitamin D: 31 mcg; Calcium: 88 mg; Iron: 2 mg; Potassium: 341 mg

BLUEBERRY BANANA PANCAKES

Makes 2 servings (7–8 pancakes)

This recipe goes way back for me. As I was delving through all of my recipes from the beginning of my alternative cooking and baking career, I stumbled across a lot of paleo and grain-free recipes. I always like to switch things up when it comes these breakfast dishes and, at the time, I was trying to find the most nutrient-dense ways to prepare them. The use of coconut flour means it will require a little extra moisture, which is why banana tends to be used when a recipe calls for this ingredient. Aside from adding an extra source of potassium, banana is a nutrient-dense alternative to regular sugar and enhances the binding capacity of the eggs when using gluten-free flours. Bananas also contain prebiotic fibers for microbial diversification in the gut, along with vitamin C and copper to help boost your immune system. Feeling like starting the day off the day with a tasty treat that boosts immunity? I'm in!

1 tbsp almond flour
3 tbsps coconut flour
1 tbsp arrowroot flour
⅛ tsp baking soda
1 tbsp flax seed (optional)

Pinch of sea salt
Stevia to taste
⅛ tsp cinnamon
3 organic, pasture-raised eggs
½ banana, mashed
¼ tsp vanilla
¼ cup full-fat coconut milk
1 cup organic blueberries
1–2 tbsps coconut oil (for cooking)

Mix all dry ingredients together in a small bowl.

In a large bowl, mash the banana and add all of the wet ingredients. With a hand beater, mix the ingredients together on medium speed until incorporated.

Continue to beat and add wet ingredients to the dry ingredients. Mix everything until incorporated.

Pour in the blueberries, fold them in the mix with a spatula, and set it aside for 3–5 minutes. This will allow the batch to thicken.

In the meantime, heat the coconut oil over medium heat in a medium-sized non-stick skillet. Wait about 2 minutes for the oil to melt and get hot.

Add the pancake mixture ¼ cup at a time. Cook for about 3 minutes and then flip. Heat this side for another minute or two. Once done, transfer to a plate and add your favorite toppings!

Guide: GF, DF, P

Nutrition Facts (1 serving)

Calories: 340; Total Fat: 21.4 g; Sat Fat: 13.7 g; Cholesterol: 246 mg; Sodium: 295 mg; Total Carbohydrates: 29.5 g; Dietary Fiber: 8.6 g; Total Sugars: 10.8 g; Protein: 11.8 g; Vitamin D: 23 mcg; Calcium: 49 mg; Iron: 2 mg; Potassium: 266 mg

HOLD THE CLUCK CHOCOLATE PANCAKES

Makes 2 servings

At one point in my food sensitivity adventures I was not only gluten and dairy-free, but also egg and grain-free. I love including pancakes in my weekend morning routines, and I refused to give that up. I was desperate and on a mission. Grain, gluten, and dairy-free are usually paleo, while egg-free is vegan. I searched for paleo pancake recipes, but most of them called for eggs. The vegan pancake recipes I found included whole wheat flour or oats. I recalled from previous culinary experiments that apple sauce is usually used as a binder in vegan recipes, while arrowroot starch acts as a binder in many paleo and gluten-free recipes. Was it possible to combine the two and make a gluten/dairy/egg/grain-free pancake? Indeed it was! Behold: I offer you a vegan, paleo pancake!

¼ cup coconut flour
¼ cup arrowroot flour
1 tsp baking soda
Pinch of salt
½ tsp cinnamon
2 tbsps cocoa powder
1 cup coconut milk

1 tbsp pure maple syrup
½ cup organic apple sauce
1 tsp apple cider vinegar
1–2 tsps almond butter
½ tablespoon coconut oil (for cooking)

Note #1: These are best done on a non-stick, BPA free pan.

Combine all dry ingredients in a large bowl and whisk them together.

In a separate smaller bowl, combine the wet ingredients and whisk them until incorporated.

Add the wet ingredients to the dry ingredients. Continuously whisk everything together until all of the ingredients are incorporated.

In a medium-sized skillet, heat the coconut oil over medium-high medium heat.

Transfer the pancake mix ¼ cup at a time onto the skillet. After about 3–5 minutes, when the top starts to slightly bubble, use a spatula to carefully flip the pancakes. Cook for another 3 minutes and transfer to a plate.

Note #2: Unfortunately, these have a tendency to fall apart. If this starts to occur, increase the heat and wait until the spatula can get a safe grip underneath them.

Guide: GF, DF, V, P

Nutrition Facts (1 serving)

Calories: 477; Total Fat: 38.8 g; Sat Fat: 30.1 g; Cholesterol: 0 mg; Sodium: 731 mg; Total Carbohydrates: 33.3 g; Dietary Fiber: 11.8 g; Total Sugars: 13.2 g; Protein: 8.1 g; Vitamin D: 0 mcg; Calcium: 41 mg; Iron: 5 mg; Potassium: 621 mg

---

PLANT-POWERED PUMPKIN PANCAKES

Makes 3–4 servings (about 8–10 pancakes)

While I was grain, gluten, egg and soy free and pumpkin season came around, I learned to use oatmeal as the base of many of my recipes and as a replacement. I wanted to stick to more whole food ingredients, rather than reaching for the all-purpose gluten-free mix. I wanted to create something that was grain-free and gluten-free, as well as vegan and egg-free. This was quite a daunting task—but I found a way to break it down and find a solution.

Flax can be substituted for eggs, while pumpkin and arrowroot starch work well as binders. The almond and coconut flour smooths the texture. Of course, with my nutritional background, I wanted everything to be packed with added health benefits. For example, flax is high in plant-based fiber; omega-3 fatty acids to help fight off inflammation; and lignans, which have been shown to decrease LDL cholesterol and help prevent cancer. You also get additional Vitamin A in the form of beta carotene from the pumpkin.

If you are looking for a smooth pancake with an autumn twist that is great for your body, I highly recommend adding this treat to a weekend morning.

½ cup almond flour
¼ cup coconut flour
¼ cup arrowroot flour
2 tsps baking powder
1 tsp pumpkin pie spice
1 tsp cinnamon
Dash of pink Himalayan sea salt
1 cup non-dairy milk
1 cup pumpkin puree
1 tbsp pure maple syrup
2 tsps vanilla extract (1 tsp if double strength)
2 tsps organic apple cider vinegar
1–2 tbsps coconut oil (for cooking)

In a medium-sized bowl, whisk together all of the dry ingredients.

In a separate medium-sized bowl, combine all of the wet ingredients and whisk them together until incorporated.

Add the dry ingredients to the wet ingredients and whisk together until fully incorporated.

Heat a large skillet over a medium flame and add the coconut oil.

Add the batter in ¼ cup portions and cover it with a flat lid. These will not bubble in the same way as traditional pancakes. Flip in about 3–4 minutes once you see the sides are cooked.

Flip and cook for another 1–2 minutes.

Transfer to a flat dish and serve with maple syrup, yogurt, and a little extra cinnamon for the garnish.

Note: These may not hold well, so it is advised that you flip with care.

Guide: GF, DF, P, V

Nutrition Facts (2 pancakes per serving)

Calories: 203; Total Fat: 14.5 g, Sat Fat: 10.5 g, Cholesterol: 0 mg; Sodium: 211 mg; Total Carbohydrates: 16.8 g; Dietary Fiber: 5.6 g; Total Sugars: 5.9 g; Protein: 3.5 g; Vitamin D: 0 mcg; Calcium: 214 mg; Iron: 3 mg; Potassium: 476 mg

GLUTEN-FREE BREAKFASTS

STRAWBERRY SHORTCAKE MORNING BUCKWHEAT

Makes 2 servings

I'm a dessert person and will find any way possible to incorporate sweet and savory flavors into my dishes. So, why not add them to gluten-free grains? Buckwheat can sometimes be bland on its own, so adding a dessert twist can make these grains much more palatable. The best part? Your body still reaps the nutritional benefits from the added magnesium. This dish also features grass-fed butter for inflammation fighting omega-3s while incorporating a pinch of savory flavor.

½ cup organic buckwheat (dry measure)
¼ tsp organic apple cider vinegar
¾ cup filtered water
¼–⅓ cup unsweetened almond milk
pinch of salt
1 cup organic strawberries
½ banana, mashed

1 tbsp grass-fed butter (or 1 tbsp coconut oil for vegan)
¼ cup full-fat coconut milk
1 packet organic stevia

Soak the buckwheat overnight in water and ¼ tsp apple cider vinegar to break down the phytic acid, which can inhibit absorption of nutrients, such as iron, calcium, and zinc. In the morning, drain and rinse it until the water is clear.

Pour water/almond milk mixture into a saucepan and bring it to boil. Note that this can boil over, so watch the pot and remove from half the heat so it does not create a mess.

Add the buckwheat, butter, strawberries, mashed banana, and stevia. Cover and turn the heat down to a simmer for 15–20 minutes.

Remove from the heat and let it stand in cover for a couple of minutes. Add the full-fat coconut milk to the mix and enjoy!

Guide: GF, DF (with coconut oil), V (with coconut oil)

Nutrition Facts (1 serving)

Calories: 326; Total Fat: 15.8 g; Sat Fat: 11.6 g; Cholesterol: 15 mg; Sodium: 93 mg; Total Carbohydrates: 44.9 g; Dietary Fiber: 7.1 g; Total Sugars: 8.3 g; Protein: 6.5 g; Vitamin D: 0 mcg; Calcium: 29 mg; Iron: 2 mg; Potassium: 428 mg

---

QI STIMULATING RASPBERRIES AND CREAM BUCKWHEAT

Makes 2 servings

I made this while trying to vitalize the qi in my body and change it up a little from a previous recipe. Dates are one of the fruits that are considered warming, and they are chock full of nutrients while adding an extra punch for a sweetener. Also, who doesn't love a little bit of tartness and creaminess? You can't go wrong with that combo.

½ cup buckwheat (or kasha)
    (dry measure)
4 dates, mashed and made into a paste
1 cup organic raspberries
1 tsp cinnamon
Dash of nutmeg
½ cup water
Salt to taste

For the Date Paste:
Note: To make the date paste, it is easier when the dates are at room temperature and soaked. De-pit the dates and place them in about 1–2 tablespoons of water. Place them in the microwave for about 15–20 seconds.

Mash the dates with a fork until a paste forms. Place it aside.

For the Dish:
Bring the water and salt to a boil. Add the buckwheat, raspberries, and cinnamon. Cover, lower the heat to low, and cook for 10–15 minutes. (*Note:* If the buckwheat expands before this time, you can add a little coconut milk. This also gives it a creamy flavor, is great for the gut and has a warming thermal nature.)

Just before the buckwheat is done, add the date paste and stir in until incorporated. For some extra creaminess, add some coconut milk.

Top with sunflower seeds if you are trying to vitalize the qi or any other delicious nuts, seeds, coconut flakes, etc. Have fun and get creative!

Note: Soak buckwheat overnight in water and a tsp of apple cider vinegar for increased nutrient bioavailability. Drain and rinse it in the morning until the water runs clear.

Guide: GF, DF, V, AI

Nutrition Facts (1 serving)

Calories: 465; Total Fat: 3.49 g; Sat Fat: .7 g; Cholesterol: 0 mg; Sodium: 93 mg; Total Carbohydrates: 78.9 g; Dietary Fiber: 13 g; Total Sugars: 36.4 g; Protein: 7.45 g; Vitamin D: 0 mcg; Calcium: 79 mg; Iron: 2.4 mg; Potassium: 594 mg

BERRIES AND CREAM MILLET

Makes 1 serving

Along my gluten-free journey, I met this little grain: millet. These pellets offer a sweeter taste than oats or buckwheat and contain a wide variety of body-loving nutrients such as fiber, magnesium, and zinc, which are beneficial for gastrointestinal health. With sweet and savory in mind, there is nothing better than a creamy berry flavor to ignite the palate in the morning. Not only is this tantalizing for your taste buds, it also offers alkalizing properties, fat-boosting and metabolism-boosting medium chain triglycerides, and cancer-fighting phytonutrients.

¼ cup millet, soaked and drained
    (dry measure)
¼ tsp organic apple cider vinegar
1–2 cups water + ½–¾ cup water
    (or non-dairy milk)
Dash of salt
¼ cup fresh organic raspberries and
    strawberries
1–2 tbsps full-fat coconut milk
Stevia to sweeten

Optional Toppings:
    Seeds
    Berries and other fruit
    Nut Butter
    Organic gluten-free granola

Measure ¼ cup of millet and soak in 1–2 cups water and apple cider vinegar overnight or for at least 8 hours. This breaks down the phytic acid that can inhibit the absorption of iron, zinc, and calcium and make the grain more digestible.

The next morning, drain and rinse the millet and put it aside.

Measure out ½–¾ cup water and add it to a saucepan with a pinch of salt. Place it on high heat until boiling and add the soaked millet, raspberries, and strawberries. Turn the heat to low, cover, and let simmer for 15 minutes.

After 15 minutes, remove the saucepan from the burner, add the full-fat coconut milk and stevia, and mix until incorporated.

Transfer to a bowl and add your choice of toppings.

Guide: GF, DF, V, AI (without nut butter)

Nutrition Facts (1 serving)

Calories: 252; Total Fat: 7.6 g; Sat Fat: 5.1 g; Cholesterol: 0 mg; Sodium: 164 mg; Total Carbohydrates: 41.4 g; Dietary Fiber: 5.5 g; Total Sugars: 2.51 g; Protein: 6.3 g; Vitamin D: 0 mcg; Calcium: 28 mg; Iron: 2 mg; Potassium: 212 mg

MILLET WITH ROASTED PARSNIPS

Makes 2 servings

I love to explore new recipes with different grains. I am also a sucker for sweet and nutty flavors. One night, while I was reading about foods that are beneficial for gut health, I stumbled upon millet and parsnips. I fell in love with both of them and thought: Why not make a functional dish that caters to the taste buds, as well as helps make my stomach happy? Not only do the flavors blend well together, but parsnips are great for their warming properties and are a rich source of several minerals—manganese, silicon, phosphorous, and potassium—which contribute not only to healthy digestive function, but also to strong bones, heart rhythm, and nerves. They are also abundant in antioxidants, such as falcarinol. This particular antioxidant has been shown to be more effective than sulforaphane from cruciferous vegetables in reducing intestinal inflammation. The best part: The effective dose of antioxidants can be attained through diet. It's no wonder I love it so much! A happy intestinal barrier equals less inflammation, which equals a thriving body.

This dish is truly a powerhouse of nutrients and flavor. I promise your taste buds and cells will enjoy every last bite.

½ cup millet (dry measure)
1–1 ½ cups hemp or coconut milk
3 medium-sized parsnips, chopped
 and mashed
2 tbsps coconut oil
¼ cup organic bone broth (vegetable
 broth for vegan)
Salt and pepper to taste

For the Parsnips:

Preheat the oven to 400°F. Peel and chop the parsnips with about ½ inch thickness. Cut large pieces of parsnip in half. Place them in a casserole dish and toss with coconut oil, bone broth, salt, and pepper until the ingredients are well combined.

Place the dish in the oven and bake until tender for about 35–45 minutes. Check on the parsnips every 15–20 minutes and stir; this allows them to cook evenly.

Remove the parsnips from the oven and place them aside.

For the Millet:

While the parsnips are baking or, for the next day, bring the non-dairy milk to a boil.

Warning! Keep an eye on this, as it may boil over.

Once boiling, place the millet in the pot and cook for about 30 minutes.

Transfer the millet to a pot and top with half a portion of the parsnips.

Guide: GF, DF, AI, V (with vegetable broth)

Nutrition Facts (1 serving)

Calories: 541; Total Fat: 22.4 g; Sat Fat: 12.2 g; Cholesterol: 0 mg; Sodium: 139 mg; Total Carbohydrates: 78.5 g; Dietary Fiber: 12.9 g; Sugars: 11.5 g; Protein: 11 g; Vitamin D: 1 mg; Calcium: 321 mg; Iron: 4 mg; Potassium: 979 mg

Note: Want to save time and a few calories? Cook the parsnips in the pot with the millet and add a pinch of coconut oil and cinnamon. It should turn out just as delectable!

GRAIN-FREE BREAKFASTS

CAROB/COCOA CHIA SEED PUDDING

Makes 1 serving

Here is a nice blend of flavors to spice up your chia seed pudding while adding in a source of some bone-loving calcium and magnesium. In terms of flavor profiles, carob provides a hearty flavor, while the chocolate adds a little bitter. It is a win-win and a nice switch-up for your average chocolate chia pudding!

3–4 tbsps full-fat coconut milk

¾ cup non-dairy milk of choice

¼ cup chia seeds

1 tbsp raw carob powder

¼ tsp apple cider vinegar

½ tsp maca powder (optional)

1 scoop vegan chocolate protein powder (optional)

In a shaker bottle—a plastic bottle containing a spherical whisk—combine the carob, coconut/non-dairy milk, maca powder, carob, and chocolate protein.

Add to a mason jar and stir in chia seeds. Add the vinegar. (This breaks down phytic acid in chia seeds, so the nutrients are more bioavailable.)

Place in the refrigerator overnight. Top with your favorite topping.

Note: Maca powder is a great addition that couples well with chocolate and can aid in recovery from strenuous exercise and help balance hormones.

Guide: GF, DF, V

Nutrition Facts (with maca powder, without protein powder) (1 serving)

Calories: 445; Total Fat: 33 g, Sat Fat: 16 g, Cholesterol: 0 mg; Sodium: 20 mg; Total Carbohydrates: 35 g; Dietary Fiber: 22.9 g; Total Sugars: 8.2 g; Protein: 14.2 g; Vitamin D: 1 mcg; Calcium: 379 mg; Iron: 3 mg; Potassium: 31 mg

ACAI CHIA SEED PUDDING

Makes 1 serving

I love having a little bit of the tropics delivered to me in a bowl. Chia seed pudding has become one of the staples in my culinary adventures, especially during times when I was completely dairy-free. I thought: I love acai bowls, so why not combine the two? This is richly packed with nutrition and so delicious! It is also simple to put together, which is ideal if you have a busy schedule.

1 packet frozen acai berry
¾ cup unsweetened coconut milk
2 tbsps chia seeds
½ banana
¼ tsp vanilla extract
Pinch of apple cider vinegar

Toppings:
¼ cup organic blueberries
1 kiwi
¼ cup organic flaked coconut

Mix all ingredients in a mason jar and let sit overnight. It's as easy as that!
Guide: GF, DF, AI, V

Nutrition Facts (1 serving)

Calories: 567; Total Fat: 37.7 g; Sat Fat: 20.1 g; Cholesterol: 0 mg; Sodium: 28 mg; Total Carbohydrates: 52.5 g; Dietary Fiber: 22.4 g; Total Sugars: 19.8 g; Protein: 9.8 g; Vitamin D: 1 mcg; Calcium: 305 mg; Iron: 4 mg; Potassium: 508 mg

---

STRAIGHT FROM THE TROPICS GREEN CHIA SEED PUDDING

Makes 1 serving

Ever long to escape to a tropical island and bring those tastes back with you to your home? That is exactly what I did with this smoothie. I created an island paradise pudding simply by combining tropical fruits and a little bit of coconut.

Kefir is a great source of gut-loving bacteria. It also provides thickness to the dish. Throwing in the greens adds extra nutrients, such as vitamin C, for antioxidant protection and magnesium and potassium to help with smooth muscle contraction. Spinach is less bitter than other greens and blends better with the flavors. Need a vacation? Incorporate this pudding into your diet.

¾ cup almond or cashew yogurt drink

3 tbsps full-fat coconut milk

1 banana

½ cup organic mango

3 large cauliflower florets, steamed

2 scoops collagen peptides (or 2 scoops plant-based protein powder for vegan)

1 tbsp chia seeds

Blend all ingredients except for the chia seeds and coconut kefir in a blender.

Once incorporated, pour the contents into a mason jar and add the chia seeds and kefir. Stir and let it sit overnight.

Note: For this recipe, I used Probiotic Dairy-Free Yogurt, Unsweetened from Califia Farm. Plain Cashewgurt (a cashew-based, dairy-free yogurt) can be another option.

Guide: GF, DF, V (replace collagen peptides with plant-based protein powder), AI

Nutrition Facts (1 serving)

Calories: 480; Total Fat: 18.6 g; Sat Fat: 8.8 g; Cholesterol: 0 mg; Sodium: 335.9.5 mg; Total Carbohydrates: 57.2 g; Dietary Fiber: 13.9 g; Total Sugars: 31.6 g; Protein: 27.1 g; Vitamin D: 0 mcg; Calcium: 169 mg; Iron: 2.2 mg; Potassium: 665 mg

OATMEAL BREAKFASTS

APPLE CINNAMON ROLLED OATS

Makes 2 servings

What is better than warm apples and spices in the morning? This is especially true for an autumn morning when you are gazing outside your window at the changing leaf colors.

Apple Cinnamon Rolled Oats are simple to prepare, yet it is a nutritious and emotionally satisfying addition to a busy morning. Apples are a great source of pectin, which helps digestive transit time, and soluble fiber, which can help lower cholesterol and feed the beneficial bacteria in your gut. Make sure to avoid apple seeds, as they can be a source of cyanide!

1 cup organic, gluten-free rolled oats

1 cup filtered water

1 cup hemp milk

1 organic Fuji apple

1 tsp cinnamon

1 pack of stevia

Pinch of pink Himalayan sea salt

Measure out the water and nut milk and pour them both into a saucepan. Add a pinch of salt and turn the flame on high until the liquid boils. In the meantime, core and chop the apple into small chunks.

When the water comes to a boil, add the oats, apples, and cinnamon. Stir until incorporated and turn the heat to low.

Cook for 10–15 minutes.

Top with flaxseed, nut butter, or any other nut or seed.

Guide: GF, DF, V, AI

Nutrition Facts (1 serving)

Calories: 384; Total Fat: 32.1 g; Sat Fat: 26 g; Cholesterol: 0 mg; Sodium: 101 mg; Total Carbohydrates: 54 g; Dietary Fiber: 12.6 g; Total Sugars: 16 g; Protein: 11.12 g; Vitamin D: 0 mcg; Calcium: 78 mg; Iron: 4.72 mg; Potassium: 692 mg

LOADED CAROB OATMEAL

Makes 1 serving

I love to make my oatmeal creamy. It adds that little extra punch as it melts in your mouth. You might ask: How do you add the creaminess without adding the cream? Simple—add some avocado! With its buttery flavor, avocado is an excellent alternative while still delivering flavor when mixed with carob. The best thing about this recipe is that not only is it loaded with body-loving nutrients for healthy bones and muscle function, it's also simple to put together.

½ cup organic, gluten-free rolled oats

1 cup filtered water

½ cup organic blueberries

¼ tsp cinnamon

Dash of nutmeg

¼ avocado

1 tbsp carob powder

1 tbsp full-fat coconut milk

1 tsp raw honey

Bring the water to a boil and add oats, blueberries, and spices. Decrease the heat to low, cover, and let simmer until oats are tender, about 10–15 minutes.

In the meantime, mash the rest of the ingredients together until they are incorporated and creamy.

Once the oats are cooked, remove them from the heat and let them stand while covered for 5 minutes.

Transfer to a bowl, mix in the avocado mash, and add your favorite nut butter.

Guide: GF, DF, V, AI

Nutrition Facts (1 serving)

Calories: 368; Total Fat: 13.1 g; Sat Fat: 4.2 g; Cholesterol: 0 mg; Sodium: 20 mg; Total Carbohydrates: 59.5 g; Dietary Fiber: 11.1 g; Total Sugars: 21.5 g; Protein: 7.8 g; Vitamin D: 0 mcg; Calcium: 80 mg; Iron: 4. mg; Potassium: 285 mg

PROTEIN APPLE CINNAMON OATMEAL

Makes 1 serving

On many occasions, my breakfast consists of pairing oatmeal with two hard-boiled eggs. I admit, though, that this tends to get boring. While I was perusing the Internet for other ways to add protein to my morning dishes, and I found a recipe that suggested adding egg whites right into the oatmeal. This made me think of baked oat breads and cakes, which usually call for eggs as part of the recipe. I reasoned that, if egg whites tasted good in those, they must also be delicious when prepared over the stove. All this requires is cracking the egg white into the oatmeal while it is cooking. The eggs give it almost a French toast-like taste. Of course, they also provide a good source of protein and B vitamins to help boost energy metabolism and decrease stress levels. This makes oatmeal even more physically nourishing and emotionally satisfying.

½ cup organic, gluten-free rolled oats
1 cup water
Dash of sea salt
1 organic apple, cored and sliced
Cinnamon
Stevia

2 organic, pasture-raised egg whites
Unsweetened almond milk to taste
Nut butter for topping (optional)

Measure out ½ cup of dried rolled oats. Fill up a pot with 1 cup of filtered water and add some sea salt.

Prepare the apple by coring and cutting it up in cubes. Toss the apple into a bowl with cinnamon and stevia and place it aside.

Heat the water until it comes to a rolling boil. Pour in the oats and add the apples. Stir in and reduce the heat to low. Set the timer for 10–15 minutes, depending on how you like your oats.

With 3 minutes left for time, crack in two egg whites, discard the yolks and shell, and stir. This will make the oatmeal extra thick.

When you are done, let cool for about 3–5 minutes.

Add your milk of choice and 1 tbsp of nut butter of choice. (Almond butter tastes best with the apple and cinnamon.)

Guide: GF, DF

Nutrition Facts (1 serving)

Calories: 307; Total Fat: 4.4 g; Sat Fat: 0 g; Cholesterol: 0 mg; Sodium: 98 mg; Total Carbohydrates: 56.1 g; Dietary Fiber: 9.3 g; Total Sugars: 17.9 g; Protein: 14.8 g; Vitamin D: 0 mcg; Calcium: 73 mg; Iron: 4 mg; Potassium: 314 mg

GOLDEN MILK STEEL CUT OATS WITH CRANBERRIES

Makes 1 serving

I recall the day I came up with this dish. It was toward the end of fall and the winter frost was starting to set in. Feeling the chill in the air and hearing some noses beginning to sniffle, I wanted to create a warming dish that featured the power of cranberries and turmeric to fight off those little pathogens and keep people healthy.

The cranberries are a great source of Vitamin C and antioxidants, which helps boost immunity. Turmeric is an excellent antiviral and antimicrobial. Combine the two and you have a dish to beat those sniffles.

¾–1 cup non-dairy milk

⅓ cup organic, gluten-free steel cut oats (dry measure)

½ cup organic cranberries

½ tsp cinnamon

¼ tsp turmeric

¼ tsp ginger

dash of cinnamon

Dash of pink Himalayan sea salt

1 tsp unrefined organic coconut oil

Stevia to taste (trust me: you will need this!)

Bring the non-dairy milk to a boil, watching carefully to avoid spill over.

Add the oats, cranberries, and coconut oil spices.

Reduce the heat to a simmer and cover.

Cook for about 20–25 minutes, stirring every 5 minutes to avoid sticking.

Note: You may need to keep adding liquid.

Remove from heat, transfer to a cereal dish, and top with your favorite nut butter.

Guide: GF, DF, AI, V

Nutrition Facts (1 serving)

Calories: 343; Total Fat: 13.3 g; Sat Fat: 7.9 g; Cholesterol: 0 mg; Sodium: 580 mg; Total Carbohydrates: 46.1 g; Dietary Fiber: 9.3 g; Total Sugars: 2 g; Protein: 8.5 g; Vitamin D: 2 mcg; Calcium: 149 mg; Iron: 3 mg; Potassium: 360 mg

---

SIMPLE AND EASY OVERNIGHT OATS

Pressed for time? These overnight oats recipes deliver nutrient density to the max. They only require mixing ingredients together and letting *them sit overnight in the refrigerator. That's it! Each dish has been created as a single serving portion catered just for you.*

PUMPKIN SPICED OVERNIGHT OATS

Makes 1 serving

When autumn rolls around, it seems that all I can think about are the pumpkin spice items that are available on the shelves.

Pumpkin spice is delicious in muffins, cupcakes, and lattes, so I thought: Why not make it into a dessert dish that is healthy and packed with nutrient potential?

Fun fact: Pumpkin is one of the highest sources of vitamin A. Not only can it help nourish your hair, skin, and nails, it may even help prevent cancer.

½ cup organic, gluten-free rolled oats
¼ cup pumpkin purée
1 tbsp organic raisins
¼ tsp pumpkin pie spice
Dash of cinnamon
¾ cup unsweetened coconut milk
1 tsp chia seeds
Stevia to taste

Guide: GF, DF, AI, V

Nutrition Facts (1 serving)

Calories: 283; Total Fat: 8.4 g; Sat Fat: 3.3 g; Cholesterol: 0 mg; Sodium: 4 mg; Total Carbohydrates: 48.2 g; Dietary Fiber: 9.7 g; Total Sugars: 7.4 g; Protein: 9 g; Vitamin D: 1 mcg; Calcium: 162 mg; Iron: 4 mg; Potassium: 261 mg

MATCHA RAISIN OVERNIGHT OATS

Makes 1 serving

Many people like to start their days in the morning with a nice hot cup of coffee or tea. Others, like me, sometimes enjoy matcha with breakfast.

Matcha is a powerhouse when it comes to nutrient potential. It is high in the antioxidant ECGC (epigallocatechin gallate) which is beneficial for liver detoxification, cancer prevention, and brain health. Add that to your oats—plus the sweetness of raisins—and you have an old-time favorite coupled with the delight of a latte!

½ cup organic, gluten-free rolled oats
½ tbsp chia seeds
1 tbsp organic raisins
½ tsp matcha green tea powder
2 scoops collagen peptides
¾ cup unsweetened coconut milk
Stevia to taste
Top with: pear and almond butter

Guide: GF, DF, AI (without almond butter)

Nutrition Facts (1 serving)

Calories: 389; Total Fat: 11 g; Sat Fat: 3.5 g; Cholesterol: 0 mg; Sodium: 220 mg; Total Carbohydrates: 47.2 g; Dietary Fiber: 12.1 g; Total Sugars: 5.4 g; Protein: 28.3 g; Vitamin D: 1 mcg; Calcium: 200 mg; Iron: 4 mg; Potassium: 111 mg

BANANA OVERNIGHT OATS

Makes 1 serving

There are times in your life when you are so busy that your creative juices become exhausted and your mind is probably fatigued as well. When that recently happened to me, I just wanted something quick that also provided a nutrient boost.

Bananas and oats contain prebiotic fibers to help feed beneficial gut bacteria, as well as vitamin B6, which may enhance your mood. Adding cinnamon increases the antioxidant content, which may help with insulin sensitivity.

When you are looking for some sanity amidst all of the chaos in your life, this dish is great to incorporate into your morning routine.

½ cup organic, gluten-free rolled oats
½ banana
½ tsp cinnamon
½ tbsp chia seeds
¾ cup non-dairy milk
Stevia to taste

Guide: GF, DF, AI, V

Nutrition Facts (1 serving)

Calories: 307; Total Fat: 9 g; Sat Fat: 3.1 g; Cholesterol: 0 mg; Sodium: 1 mg; Total Carbohydrates: 52.3 g; Dietary Fiber: 12.3 g; Total Sugars: 7.3 g; Protein: 9.2 g; Vitamin D: 1 mcg; Calcium: 172 mg; Iron: 4 mg; Potassium: 251 mg

CARROT CAKE OVERNIGHT ZOATS

Makes 1 serving

Many nutritionists believe that, in order for our body to function optimally, we need to eat at least 2 servings of fruits and 7–9 servings of vegetables a day. If you generally enjoy three solid meals, why not include some of the fruit and vegetable requirements right in your breakfast routine?

This Carrot Cake Overnight Zoats recipe provides ¼ serving of fruit and almost 2 servings of vegetables. The zucchini and carrots are excellent sources of carotenoids, which help with healthy hair, skin, and nails. The banana helps to boost dopamine levels, which may improve your focus. Your body and your taste buds will truly be thanking you after consuming this dish. I know mine do!

½ cup organic, gluten-free rolled oats
¼ cup organic zucchini, shaved
¼ cup organic carrots, shaved
½ banana, mashed
½ tsp cinnamon
¼ tsp nutmeg
¼ tsp ginger spice
½ tbsp chia seeds
1 tbsp organic raisins (optional)
¾ cup unsweetened coconut milk

Guide: GF, DF, AI, V

Nutrition Facts (with raisins)
(1 serving)

Calories: 380 Total Fat: 9.5 g; Sat Fat: 3.3 g; Cholesterol: 0 mg; Sodium: 53 mg; Total Carbohydrates: 70.2 g; Dietary Fiber: 14 g; Total Sugars: 19.6 g; Protein: 11.9 g; Vitamin D: 0 mcg; Calcium: 192 mg; Iron: 4 mg; Potassium: 946 mg

APPLE CINNAMON GOLDEN MILK OVERNIGHT OATS

Makes 1 serving

I often love combining a variety of flavors into one dish. Pumpkin spice and apple spice are two of my favorites, especially in the autumn.

Along with fall and the change in seasons comes a rise in colds and flu. One of my go-tos when I'm feeling rundown is to reach for a glass of golden milk, which is high in antioxidants and contains antibacterial, antiviral, and antifungal properties.

½ cup organic, gluten-free rolled oats

½ tsp cinnamon

¼ tsp turmeric

¼ tsp ginger

1 tbsp organic raisins

¾ cup unsweetened coconut milk

1 tsp chia seeds

1 tbsp gold flaxseed meal

1 organic small apple, cored and diced

Stevia to taste

Guide: GF, DF, AI, V

Nutrition Facts (1 serving)

Calories: 376; Total Fat: 9.9 g; Sat Fat: 3.2 g; Cholesterol: 0 mg; Sodium: 1 mg; Total Carbohydrates: 68.2 g; Dietary Fiber: 16.2 g; Total Sugars: 22.2 g; Protein: 9.9 g; Vitamin D: 0 mcg; Calcium: 143 mg; Iron: 15 mg; Potassium: 318 mg

PEPPERMINT MOCHA CAFFEINE-FREE OVERNIGHT OATS

Makes 1 serving

During the holiday season, I like to incorporate a festive flavor into my overnight oats. One of my favorite winter delicacies is peppermint mocha. I wanted to create a caffeine-free version of this, so I swapped in decaf coffee and used toasted carob powder in place of chocolate. Carob is not just a chocolate replacement for several recipes, it is an excellent source of fiber and plant-based calcium to strengthen your bones.

The best part? You get a two-for-one deal (coffee and oats) with this dish. Place the peppermint mocha in a mason jar, add in some oats and chia seeds, and let it sit overnight in the fridge.

½ cup organic, gluten-free rolled oats
6 oz organic decaf coffee
1 heaping tbsp carob powder
1 scoop collagen peptides
2–3 tbsps full-fat coconut milk
1 tbsp chia seeds
¼ tsp organic peppermint extract
Stevia to taste

Guide: GF, DF

Nutrition Facts (1 serving)

Calories: 382; Total Fat: 13.5 g; Sat Fat: 6 g; Cholesterol: 0 mg; Sodium: 141 mg; Total Carbohydrates: 48.6 g; Dietary Fiber: 12.8 g; Total Sugars: 7.1 g; Protein: 21.6 g; Vitamin D: 0 mcg; Calcium: 163 mg; Iron: 4 mg; Potassium: 579 mg

SMOOTHIE RECIPES

Whether you are on the go or would like to add more variety to your diet, smoothies can be a great *starter for your day. It can also be a daytime snack, a post-workout recovery drink, or even a dessert.*

THE BASIC

Makes 1 serving

This is probably the most common green smoothie recipe I have come across. It also happens to be the first green smoothie I dabbled with while I was on my nutrition journey and continues to be a staple for me when I want something simple, satisfying, and full of nutrients. The blueberries provide a great source of antioxidants, while the bananas contain vitamin B6, which can improve your mood and do wonders for your brain.

1 cup organic spinach

1 cup organic blueberries

½ banana

2 tbsps ground flaxseed

1 tbsp almond butter

¾ cup unsweetened almond milk

¾ cup ice

Note: Can't have nuts or peanuts? Switch to coconut milk in place of almond milk and sunflower seed butter instead of almond butter.

Add all ingredients to a blender and process until incorporated.

Guide: GF, DF, V, P

Nutrition Facts (1 serving)

Calories: 324; Total Fat: 15.7 g; Sat Fat: 1.1 g; Cholesterol: 0 mg; Sodium: 168 mg; Total Carbohydrates: 44.8 g; Dietary Fiber: 11.2 g; Total Sugars: 22.8 g; Protein: 10.4 g; Vitamin D: 1 mcg; Calcium: 119 mg; Iron: 4 mg; Potassium: 520 mg

---

BEET AND BERRY SMOOTHIE

Makes 1 serving

This is a great smoothie for an antioxidant punch, as well as for liver health. Beets are one of the best blood tonics out there and also gives this dish its vibrant color.

½ cup cooked beets, cubed
1 cup organic mixed berries
¾ cups coconut milk
2 tbsps almond butter
Stevia to taste

Note: If you are not using frozen berries, add ice for thickness.

Add all ingredients to a blender and process until incorporated.
Guide: GF, DF, V, P

Nutrition Facts (1 serving)

Calories: 347; Total Fat: 22 g; Sat Fat: 4.4 g; Cholesterol: 0 mg; Sodium: 67 mg; Total Carbohydrates: 33 g; Dietary Fiber: 10.7 g; Total Sugars: 18.2 g; Protein: 9.2 g; Vitamin D: 1 mcg; Calcium: 119 mg; Iron: 7 mg; Potassium: 709 mg

---

CHOCO-BERRY GREEN SMOOTHIE

Makes 1 serving

Chocolate and berries are always a win-win combination. It makes me think of those Brookside Chocolate Covered fruits. Not only is this smoothie satisfying to the taste buds, it offers antioxidants that may help with cognition, muscle recovery, and joint health!

¾ cup unsweetened coconut milk

1 scoop chocolate vegan protein powder (or 1 tbsp cocoa powder)

1 scoop collagen peptides

1 tbsp organic, gluten-free rolled oats

½ cup organic blueberries, frozen

½ cup organic strawberries, frozen

1 cup organic spinach

1 heaping tsp almond butter

1 tbsp golden flax seed

Stevia to taste

Add all ingredients to a blender and process until incorporated.

Guide: GF, DF

Note: Make this into a functional smoothie bowl! Top with hemp seeds, coconut flakes, pear slices and nut butter of choice.

Nutrition Facts (without protein powder) (1 serving)

Calories: 212; Total Fat: 6.5 g; Sat Fat: 3.8 g; Cholesterol: 0 mg; Sodium: 133 mg; Total Carbohydrates: 28.1 g; Dietary Fiber: 8.9 g; Total Sugars: 11.8 g; Protein: 12.6 g; Vitamin D: 1 mcg; Calcium: 128 mg; Iron: 3 mg; Potassium: 272 mg

ANTIOXIDANT PUNCH SMOOTHIE

Makes 1 serving

Just as the recipe name says, this smoothie is loaded with antioxidants. The camu camu powder is one of the highest sources of vitamin C, delivering around 750% of your DV (daily value), which can help keep your immune system healthy. Another plus? It's incredibly simple to put together.

¾ cup unsweetened almond milk
1 tsp camu camu powder
1 cup organic blueberries
1 cup organic spinach
1 tbsp sunflower butter
Stevia to taste

Add all ingredients to a blender and process until incorporated.

Guide: GF, DF, V, P

Nutrition Facts (1 serving)

Calories: 230; Total Fat: 10.5 g; Sat Fat: 0.8 g; Cholesterol: 0 mg; Sodium: 176 mg; Total Carbohydrates: 32.9 g; Dietary Fiber: 4.2 g; Total Sugars: 14.5 g; Protein: 5.9 g; Vitamin D: 1 mcg; Calcium: 66 mg; Iron: 4 mg; Potassium: 322 mg

CHOCOLATE PB&J SMOOTHIE BOWL

This takes the idea of Reese's Peanut Butter Cups and adds a little tart flavor for the taste buds to savor. The best part? It's free of the refined sugars, yet high in antioxidants and fiber.

½ cup unsweetened coconut milk
(use ¾ cup if making a smoothie
instead of a smoothie bowl)
1 tbsp organic peanut butter
¾ cup organic red grapes
2 scoops vegan chocolate protein powder
(or 2 tbsps cocoa powder)
1 tbsp organic, gluten-free rolled oats
Top with: coconut, plums, and hemp
seeds

Add all ingredients to a blender and process until incorporated.

Guide: GF, DF, V

> **Nutrition Facts (1 serving)**
>
> Calories: 221; Total Fat: 11.4 g; Sat Fat: 3.8 g; Cholesterol: 0 mg; Sodium: 74 mg; Total Carbohydrates: 24.1 g; Dietary Fiber: 4.7 g; Total Sugars: 10.6 g; Protein: 7.4 g; Vitamin D: 1 mcg; Calcium: 54 mg; Iron: 4 mg; Potassium: 429 mg

ANTIOXIDANT BOOSTER SMOOTHIE

Makes 1 serving

Want some to add some creamy thickness to your shake? This recipe uses avocado to provide the beverage with a smooth texture and to further add a source of free radical scavenging antioxidants. Usually collagen is touted for benefitting hair and skin, but it also contains an amino acid known as glycine, which may help to increase your body's natural antioxidant, glutathione. A high amount of antioxidants in your body may help to heighten energy and improve brain function, which is a recipe for success to take on the day!

¾ cup unsweetened coconut milk
1 scoop collagen peptides
½ cup organic blueberries
½ cup organic strawberries
½ banana
1 cup organic spinach
½ avocado
1 tsp maca powder
2 tbsps organic apple juice

Add all ingredients to a blender and process until incorporated.

Guide: GF, DF, AI, P

Nutrition Facts (1 serving)

Calories: 420; Total Fat: 23.4 g; Sat Fat: 7.2 g; Cholesterol: 0 mg; Sodium: 141 mg; Total Carbohydrates: 45.2 g; Dietary Fiber: 13.3 g; Total Sugars: 21.9 g; Protein: 13.8 g; Vitamin D: 1 mcg; Calcium: 142 mg; Iron: 3 mg; Potassium: 1093 mg

---

POTASSIUM PUNCH GREEN SMOOTHIE

Makes 1 serving

Our diets are constantly bombarded by loads of sodium, yet we tend to be deficient in the other electrolyte: potassium. Did you know that these two actually work together—in particular, for healthy heart rhythm?

This sweet, tropical smoothie contains almost ⅓ of the Daily Recommended Value of potassium, which not only may help with proper heart function but also can improve bone strength and muscle function.

1 cup organic spinach
½ banana
¼ medium cantaloupe
1 cup unsweetened coconut milk
¼ avocado
1 tsp coconut oil

Handful of ice
1–2 scoops vegan vanilla protein powder (optional)

Add all ingredients to a blender and process until incorporated.

Guide: GF, DF, AI, V, P (without vegan protein powder)

> **Nutrition Facts (without protein powder) (1 serving)**
>
> Calories: 293; Total Fat: 18.9 g; Sat Fat: 10.1 g; Cholesterol: 0 mg; Sodium: 49 mg; Total Carbohydrates: 32.2 g; Dietary Fiber: 7.8 g; Total Sugars: 18.5 g; Protein: 3.6 g; Vitamin D: 2 mcg; Calcium: 152 mg; Iron: 2 mg; Potassium: 1031 mg

HAPPY HORMONE BERRY PUNCH

Makes 1 serving

This smoothie contains maca powder, which is known as an adaptogenic herb—a component that helps your body cope with everyday demands. In turn, this may help improve immunity, fight off damaging free radicals, and balance out hormones. When your hormones are happy, your body and mind are happy as well.

The ingredients in this recipe are satisfying to the taste buds and may uplift your mood, as chocolate can increase dopamine levels. It's a win-win and a great way to ease into the day. If you are using this post-workout, which I normally do, the addition of a vanilla protein powder adds an excellent muscle-building component.

1 cup non-dairy milk
½ cup organic blueberries
½ cup organic dark cherries
2 tbsps raw cacao powder
1 tsp maca powder
½–1 tsp cinnamon
1 tbsp almond butter
Stevia to taste
1 scoop vegan vanilla protein powder (optional)

Add all ingredients to a blender and process until incorporated.

Guide: GF, DF, V, P (without vegan protein powder)

Nutrition Facts (without protein powder) (1 serving)

Calories: 321; Total Fat: 14.8 g; Sat Fat: 1 g; Cholesterol: 0 mg; Sodium: 182 mg; Total Carbohydrates: 41 g; Dietary Fiber: 10.2 g; Total Sugars: 18.2 g; Protein: 11.12 g; Vitamin D: 1 mcg; Calcium: 312 mg; Iron: 8 mg; Potassium: 714 mg

DINNERS

MAIN COURSES

BODY WARMING SAUTÉED CHICKPEA STUFFED ACORN SQUASH

Makes 3–4 servings

I love this dish so much I had to share it on a local TV appearance. I was inspired to create this recipe by the warming food energetics of the ingredients. According to Traditional Chinese Medicine, foods such as chickpeas, squashes, and sesame seeds are warming to the body, which may in turn help calm your system down and heat up those areas that are cold. With these properties in mind, this makes a wonderful autumnal dish. Plus, it is easy to put together, which makes it a great option for a busy night.

2 cups cooked chickpeas, drained and rinsed
3–4 cups organic raw spinach
1 red onion
4 bulbs garlic, mashed and chopped
½ tsp cumin

1 tbsp sesame seeds
2 tbsps grapeseed oil
1 medium acorn squash (seeded and halved)
2 tsps grass-fed butter (or coconut oil)
½ tsp cinnamon (divided)
Salt and pepper

Preheat the oven to 375°F.

Halve and seed one acorn squash and place in a 9 x 12 baking dish. Rub it with butter and add spices, salt, and pepper. Bake for 45 minutes.

Mash garlic and chop onions. Let it sit for 5 minutes.

Pour the grapeseed oil into to a skillet over medium heat. Add the onions and cook them until they are translucent (about 3 minutes). Toss in the spinach, garlic, and chickpeas and mix everything together. Once the spinach is cooked, add the sesame seeds and cumin. Decrease the heat and cook for another 5 minutes.

After 45 minutes, remove the acorn squash and stuff it with the sautéed chickpeas. Place it back in the oven for another 5–10 minutes.

Guide: GF, DF (with coconut oil), AI (with coconut oil), V (with coconut oil)

Nutrition Facts (1 serving)

Calories: 302; Total Fat: 12.2 g, Sat Fat: 2.4 g, Cholesterol: 5 mg; Sodium: 245 mg; Total Carbohydrates: 41.3 g; Dietary Fiber: 9.6 g; Total Sugars: 5.3 g; Protein: 9.8 g; Vitamin D: 0 mcg; Calcium: 139 mg; Iron: 5 mg; Potassium: 837 mg

PASTA WITH CHICKPEAS, SPINACH, AND PUMPKIN SAGE CREAM SAUCE

Makes 2 servings

In previous recipes, I commented about how much I love the fall and how much flavor you can bring to dishes during that particular season. One evening, while I was alone and had the freedom to create my own mini-kitchen adventure, I arrived at this dish.

I love both pumpkin and cream sauces and sought a way to combine these flavors. I began by experimenting with cauliflower to add creaminess to my dishes. Meanwhile, coconut milk had been a longtime staple substitution for cream. I mixed the cauliflower and coconut milk and—voilà—this idea was birthed! I admit I had to indulge in a second helping of the sauce.

Though this dish is considered carb-heavy (nearly 90 grams per serving), it contains about 60% of the daily recommended serving of fiber, which is beneficial for colonic transit and feeding beneficial bacteria.

Other ingredients, such as pumpkin, are high in beta carotene, which helps with skin, hair, and nail health and acts as a potent antioxidant to help the body fight against cancer. Meanwhile, cauliflower is part of the cruciferous vegetable family, *which aids in improving liver detoxification and makes the toxins in your system more water soluble so they don't float around your body. This is an opportunity to cleanse your body of toxins while your taste buds enjoy the autumn notes.*

4 oz gluten-free pasta
1 can organic garbanzo beans
2–3 cups organic spinach raw
    (1–1 ½ cups cooked)

For the Sauce:

1 cup pumpkin purée
3 tbsps organic tomato sauce
3 tbsps full-fat coconut milk
½ cup cauliflower, steamed
2 fresh sage leaves
Dash of cinnamon
Salt and pepper to taste

Boil the pasta according to the instructions on the package or box. Once the noodles are ready, drain them and place them back in the pot.

While the pasta is cooking, lightly steam the spinach and cauliflower for 5 minutes. Place it aside.

In the meantime, mix the pumpkin, coconut milk, tomato sauce, and cinnamon together in a saucepan until the ingredients are incorporated. Add ½ cup steamed cauliflower and sage to the saucepan and mix with a hand blender until liquified. Cook the mixture over light heat to warm it up, about 3 minutes.

In the pot with the pasta, add the chickpeas, spinach, and ½ pumpkin sage cream sauce and mix everything together.

Note #1: Add a dash of non-dairy milk if the sauce is too thick.

Guide: GF, DF, AI (without tomato sauce), V

> **Nutrition Facts (1 serving)**
>
> Calories: 477; Total Fat: 5.3 g, Sat Fat: 1.5 g, Cholesterol: 0 mg; Sodium: 178 mg; Total Carbohydrates: 89.8 g; Dietary Fiber: 15.1 g; Total Sugars: 7 g; Protein: 17.5 g; Vitamin D: 0 mcg; Calcium: 177 mg; Iron: 6 mg; Potassium: 899 mg

Note #2: Want to leave out the tomato if you have a sensitivity to nightshades, vegetables of the *Solanacea* family, that may aggravate joint pain and arthritis? Replace the 3 tbsps of tomato sauce with 3 tbsps of pumpkin puree.

SWEET COCONUT CURRIED CHICKPEAS

Makes 2–3 servings

Curry is one of my absolute favorite dishes, but I found it difficult to incorporate in a diet that is free of nightshades, vegetables of the Solanacea family, such as tomatoes, eggplant and potatoes that may aggravate joint pain or arthritis pain among sensitive individuals. As the cliché goes: When there is a will there is a way, correct? I became determined to figure it out and ended up with this excellent recipe.

Sweet Coconut Curried Chickpeas are great for those nights when it is cold out and you'd like a nice warming dish—or when you want to add a little spice into your night.

Trust me: There is no wrong way to have curry. The best part? Curry contains turmeric, which has active compounds to help kill cancer cells, decrease oxidative stress, and protect the body against harmful bacteria.

1 yellow onion, diced
1 ½ tbsps coconut oil
4–5 garlic bulbs
1 tsp curry spice
¼ tsp turmeric
½ tsp coriander
½ tsp cumin
½ tsp black pepper
Salt
½ cup organic chicken stock or bone
    broth (vegetable stock for vegan)
6 tbsps full-fat coconut milk
½ lemon, juiced
1 can (about 1 ¾ cups) organic chickpeas

Crush the garlic and let it sit for 5 minutes. Finely chop the pieces and then do the same for the yellow onion.

Add the coconut oil to the skillet and cook over medium heat. Once it is hot (about 3 minutes), add the chopped onion and garlic. Cook until it smells fragrant (about 2–3 minutes).

Drain and rinse the chickpeas. Add them to the skillet, along with all the spices. Cook for about 5 minutes.

Add the broth, coconut milk, and lemon. Turn heat down to low flame and let simmer for about 10 minutes.

Enjoy over rice or cauliflower rice!
Guide: GF, DF, V (with vegetable stock)

Nutrition Facts (1 serving)

Calories: 387; Total Fat: 14.4 g; Sat Fat: 10.9 g; Cholesterol: 0 mg; Sodium: 160 mg; Total Carbohydrates: 46.7 g; Dietary Fiber: 11.1 g; Total Sugars: 6.4 g; Protein: 16.5 g; Vitamin D: 0 mcg; Calcium: 126 mg; Iron: 3 mg; Potassium: 541 mg

GIMME SOME SPICE VEGAN CHILI

Makes about 12 servings

When it comes to creating a meal that is chock full of nutrients, chili is one of the finest options. The best part? You can make it however you like!

6 small (or 3 large) celery sticks, chopped
2 tbsps chili powder
½ tbsp cinnamon
1 tbsp ground cumin
1 ½ tsps salt
1 ½ cups organic corn niblets
1 ½ cups chopped fresh cilantro

On a cutting board, dice up the onions and the garlic.

Note: Make sure you crush the garlic and wait at least 5 minutes before chopping. This allows the cancer-fighting constituent allicin to be activated.

Place 4 large carrots into a food processor and blend until finely shredded."

In a large pot, heat the 2 tbsps of olive oil over medium heat. Wait about 2–3 minutes. Add the onions and garlic and cook until they are translucent.

Add all of the other ingredients except for the tomatoes. Mix and cook them for 3–4 more minutes. Add in the diced tomatoes and increase the heat to high. Once the liquid is

boiling, turn the heat to low and bring it to a simmer. Let it cook 30–40 minutes.

Top with fresh cilantro, avocado, or even egg!

Guide: GF, DF, V

ONE CLASSY QUESADILLA

Makes 1 serving

High end cafes and luncheons often feature dishes that include pesto with spinach or some other vegetables. Pesto is one of my absolute favorite sauces, and it is incredibly good for you!

While preparing a quesadilla one evening, I decided to include a pesto sauce with even more nutrient-packed vegetables. One of my favorite veggies to add to sandwiches—and pretty much everything else—is beets!

This combination was so delicious it reminded me of a classy panini that you might order in a New York City restaurant. At the time, I was also gluten and dairy-free, so I decided to give myself an extra treat by using some alternative cheese and tortillas.

For the Quesadilla:

½ tbsp coconut oil
2 Siete cassava and coconut flour tortillas
¼ cup Daiya dairy-free cheese shreds
2 small cooked beets
1 handful organic spinach
1 tbsp *dairy-free pesto*

For the Pesto:

2 cloves of garlic
¼ cup extra virgin olive oil
½ cup pine nuts, toasted
3 cups fresh basil leaves
¼ tsp pink Himalayan Sea Salt

For the Pesto:

Preheat the oven on 250°F.

Pour the pine nuts in a pie pan lined with parchment paper and place them to the oven. Bake for about 10 minutes, checking every two minutes to avoid burning them.

Wash basil leaves and remove stems.

Place garlic cloves in a food processor and pulse for 10 seconds until minced.

Place the 3 cups of basil leaves in the food processor and blend until the leaves and garlic until a puree forms.

Add the toasted pine nuts and process until they are mixed thoroughly with basil and garlic puree.

Add the sea salt and olive oil through the feed tube and continue to process until all the ingredients are incorporated. Place aside.

For the Quesadilla:

Add the oil to a skillet and heat over medium heat.

Cut the beets in half and length-wise.

Place a tortilla on the skillet and add all ingredients on top.

Cover the ingredients with the second tortilla and smear some oil on the outside. Place a lid over the skillet to contain the heat and melt the dairy-free cheese faster. Cook for about 5–8 minutes or until the cheese is almost melted. Once it's ready, flip the quesadilla carefully. Cook for another 3–5 minutes.

Guide: GF, DF, V, P

> **Nutrition Facts (1 serving)**
>
> Calories: 355; Total Fat: 20 g; Sat Fat: 11 g; Cholesterol: 0 mg; Sodium: 846 mg; Total Carbohydrates: 39 g; Dietary Fiber: 6 g; Total Sugars: 4 g; Protein: 4 g; Vitamin D: 0 mcg; Calcium: 80 mg; Iron: 2 mg; Potassium: 273 mg

PALEO FIESTA FISH TACOS

Makes 7–8 servings

When I am in need of something fresh and nutritious, fish tacos are one of my favorite go-to meals. On the surface, you might not consider fish tacos nutritious. However, if you think about it, you can top a taco with all kinds of vegetables, and there are so many different varieties you can choose from.

While sitting in bed one night, I contemplated how to make a grain-free, paleo-friendly taco that was loaded with vegetables and extra nutrients. Inspired by Chipotle's lime cilantro rice, I decided to put my own twist on it and replace the rice with cauliflower. Cauliflower is a cruciferous vegetable that is great for Phase 2 liver detoxification, a process in the liver which makes toxins water soluble so they can be eliminated through the urine.

This dish is also packed with anti-inflammatory omega-3 fatty acids DHA, EPA, and Alpha Linolenic Acid, while delivering fiber, beta carotene, and vitamin B6 for colon health, radiant hair skin and nails, and a boost in your mood. (I can personally attest to this.) Not only are you delivering a nutrient powerhouse to your body with this meal, but your taste buds will be thanking you as well.

16 oz fresh wild caught cod

1 lemon, juiced

1 cup sweet potatoes, cubed in ½ inch squares

1 medium avocado, diced

Salt and pepper

3 ½ cups riced cauliflower

1 tbsp fresh lime juice

½ cup cilantro

1–1 ½ tbsps coconut oil

Salt and pepper to taste

7–8 coconut flour or organic corn tortillas

Line a pan with aluminum foil and coat it with coconut oil. Place the fish on top and sprinkle it with salt, pepper, and lemon juice. Let it sit for 5–10 minutes to allow the fish to marinate.

Set the oven to broil. Place the fish in the oven and cook it until completely white (about 5–10 minutes).

For the Cauliflower:

Heat the coconut oil over medium to medium-high flame. Add the cauliflower rice, lime juice, cilantro, salt, and pepper. Toss the ingredients until they are incorporated and cook until the rice is tender (about 5 minutes). Place it aside.

In the meantime, place the chopped sweet potatoes in a steamer and heat them until tender. Since they are small, this should only take about 5 minutes.

Place the tortillas on a large plate. Add the fish, followed but the cauliflower, avocado, and sweet potatoes. Top with fresh cilantro for a garnish.

Guide: GF, DF, AI (with coconut flour tortillas), P (with coconut flour tortillas)

Nutrition Facts (1 serving)

Calories: 172; Total Fat: 6.9 g, Sat Fat: 3.5 g, Cholesterol: 22.5 mg; Sodium: 266.7 mg; Total Carbohydrates: 16.8 g; Dietary Fiber: 5.3 g; Total Sugars: 2.4 g; Protein: 12.4 g; Vitamin D: 0 mcg; Calcium: 109 mg; Iron: 1 mg; Potassium: 427.2 mg

SAUTÉED HERB BUTTERNUT SQUASH, CHICKPEAS, SPINACH OVER ZUCCHINI NOODLES

Makes 1 serving

On arriving home one day towards the end of summer, I scavenged my refrigerator and cabinets in search of what I could assemble for dinner. I wanted something quick yet packed with nutrients from veggies. I also wanted to incorporate herbs into the dish, so I looked up what went well with the butternut squash I found in the refrigerator.

Not only is this dish easy to put together, it is high in fiber, which helps support healthy gut bacteria.

1 medium organic zucchini, spiralized
¾ cup butternut squash, cubed
2 cups organic baby spinach
¾ cup cooked organic chickpeas
3 leaves fresh sage
5 sprigs fresh thyme
2 sprigs fresh rosemary
½–¾ cup organic bone broth (vegetable stock for vegan)

1 tbsp organic tahini
Salt and pepper to taste

With a spiralizer, process the zucchini into *zoodles*—long strands of zucchini resembling spaghetti noodles.

Place ¾ cup of cubed butternut squash into a steamer. Cook until it is almost soft enough to poke a fork through (about 20 minutes).

In a medium skillet, heat the bone broth over medium heat. Add the spinach and cook until almost wilted (about 2 minutes). Add the chickpeas, butternut squash, herbs, salt, and pepper, tossing them until they are incorporated. Cook for about 2 minutes and push aside, so half the pan is free. Pour in the zoodles and toss them around without touching the other ingredients. Cook until just tender (about 2 minutes).

Transfer to a bowl and top with the tahini.

Note: The bone broth may evaporate. Continue to monitor it and add more, if need be.

Guide: GF, DF, AI, V (with vegetable stock)

SAUTÉED BUTTERNUT, BRUSSELS, AND GARLIC SALMON MEDLEY OVER SWEET POTATO SPIRALS

Makes 2 servings

Have you ever had those days when you know you have a lot of nutritious ingredients, but you are faced with two challenges—creativity and time? This dish was originated while I faced those two constraints. I was trying to stay away from grains and was craving more of a noodle dish. Instead of zucchini noodles, I decided to spiralize a sweet potato.

What I love so much about this dish is the alkalinity it delivers from the array of fruits and vegetables. The garlic consists of several cancer fighting compounds, such as allicin, prebiotic fibers to feed beneficial bacteria, and possesses antimicrobial, antifungal, and antiviral properties that are essential for the winter months. The Brussels sprouts add in the sulfur component, which helps rid the body of harmful toxins. With a little herbal twist, this dish not only delivers an array of body-loving nutrients, it works with your budget of time and delivers an array of flavors for your palate to savor.

1–2 tbsps extra virgin olive oil
8 oz sweet potato, spiralized
½ cup butternut squash, cubed
½ cup organic Brussels sprouts, cut in halves
2 large garlic bulbs, minced
Dash of sage
Dash of savory
Dash of thyme
6 oz wild caught salmon
Salt and pepper to taste

Cut off the ends of the sweet potato and then slice it in half, width wise. With a spiralizer, process the sweet potatoes and place them aside.

Steam the butternut squash and Brussels sprouts in steamer and cook until they are almost tender.

Heat the olive oil in a skillet over medium heat. Add the steamed veggies to one side of the skillet and the sweet potatoes to the other.

Add the herbs, salt, and pepper to the steamed veggies, along with the fish and garlic. Heat the fish on one side until it is cooked (about 3 minutes), flip it, and chop it into pieces with a spatula.

Add the salt and pepper to the sweet potatoes.

Note: Keep these separate from the other medley!

Continue to cook until the salmon is no longer pink and all of the veggies are tender (about 5 minutes).

Remove the sweet potato spirals first, placing them in a bowl and topping them with the medley.

Guide: GF, DF, AI, P

Nutrition Facts (1 serving)

Calories: 372; Total Fat: 19 g, Sat Fat: 2.8 g, Cholesterol: 47 mg; Sodium: 178 mg; Total Carbohydrates: 30.67 g; Dietary Fiber: 5.4 g; Total Sugars: 8.63 g; Protein: 20.45 g; Vitamin D: 217 IU; Calcium: 89 mg; Iron: 2.3 mg; Potassium: 1178 mg

ADZUKI AVO PASTA

Makes 1 serving

This recipe originated while I was becoming somewhat obsessed with learning about the healing properties of food from Paul Pitchford's book Healing with Whole Foods.

Adzuki beans and brown rice are known for drying "damp" conditions in the body. This means they help with digestion and warming the body. (At the time my digestion was sluggish and I tended to be more on the cold side.)

I try to incorporate the avocado as a staple in as many dishes as possible. Also, I love Mexican-style dishes of rice and beans that often feature guacamole—one of the best foods for you—on the side. All of the ingredients in guacamole are healthy: cilantro helps to bind heavy metals; red onions are a great source of quercetin, an antioxidant that helps detox carcinogens; and avocados contain vitamin B6, boron, magnesium, potassium, and alpha linolenic acid, which are beneficial for mood, sex hormone production, proper heart rhythm, and inflammation.

As a side note, this was a team effort with my mother that has since become a favorite dish for both of us.

1 cup brown rice or quinoa pasta
(about 2 oz)
½ avocado
1 tsp organic apple cider vinegar
½ clove garlic, crushed (or dash
of garlic powder)
½ small onion, diced
½ tbsp of extra virgin olive oil
Salt and pepper to taste
½ cup organic canned adzuki beans

Note: To cut down the calories, use half of the avocado sauce and save some for the following day.

Cook the pasta according to the directions on the package or box.

Toss the onions and garlic in a blender or mini-food processor. Process them until they are well-chopped. Add in the avocado, apple cider vinegar, olive oil, salt and pepper and process until all ingredients are incorporated.

Drain and rinse the adzuki beans and add them with the avocado sauce to the brown rice pasta.

Mix all together and enjoy!

Guide: GF, DF, AI, V

NIGHTSHADE-FREE CURRIED LENTILS

Makes 2–3 servings

I love curry spices, but for a while I was unable to tolerate nightshades, such as peppers, paprika, and tomatoes, as they would create some joint pain. Even so, I became determined to find ways to prepare curry, especially because of the healing benefits of turmeric. As you'll note in this recipe, I found a way to utilize the wonderful spices found in a curry mix, but without the pesky nightshades.

½ cup red lentils (dry measure)

10 organic baby carrots (or 2 large carrots), grated

¼–½ cup onion, chopped

4 cloves garlic, minced

2 tbsps grapeseed, coconut, or extra virgin olive oil

1–1 ½ cups filtered water (or broth)

½ tsp turmeric

½ tsp cumin

½ tsp coriander

Pinch of cinnamon

Salt and pepper to taste

Optional:

To reduce cooking time and facilitate the best absorption, assimilation, and digestion of the nutrients, soak the lentils in water and 1 tsp apple cider vinegar for 8–12 hours. Make sure to fully rinse the lentils prior to cooking.

For the Recipe:

Crush and chop the garlic (releasing the cancer-fighting components) and onions. Add the carrots to a food processor and process them until they are in small pieces.

Heat the oil in a medium pot over medium heat. Once hot enough, add the onions and garlic together and cook for about 2 minutes. Add the carrots and cook them for about 2 minutes. Sprinkle in and mix the spices, salt, and pepper. Add in the dried lentils and mix them with the other ingredients.

Once everything is incorporated, add 1 cup of the filtered water (or broth) and turn the heat to high. Once it boils, turn the heat down to low and simmer for about 15–20 minutes. Continue to stir every

2 minutes and keep an eye on the water level. After about 5 minutes, add another ½ cup of water (or broth) and raise the heat to low-medium for 2 minutes—just to warm up the liquid.

Remove it from the heat and enjoy!

Guide: GF, DF, V, AI

Calories: 338; Total Fat: 14.7 g; Sat Fat: 2.1 g; Cholesterol: 0 mg; Sodium: 74 mg; Total Carbohydrates: 40 g; Dietary Fiber: 17.1 g; Total Sugars: 5.2 g; Protein: 13.7 g; Vitamin D: 0 mcg; Calcium: 76 mg; Iron: 5 mg; Potassium: 760 mg

CURRIED CHICKEN STUFFED SQUASH

Makes 4 servings

When the weather gets cold, meat and squash dishes are my go-to, especially if it involves stuffing the meat into the squash and baking it. I had been "currying" pretty much everything at the time, and I experimented with a new squash, the delicata squash.

This recipe can be prepared with minimal effort. The curry helps to kill unwanted germs in your body, and the dish will make you feel warm and cozy. If you happen to have a fireplace, light it up and enjoy this meal in front of the flames.

For the Squash:

2 squash, cut in half and seeded
1 tsp grass-fed butter (or coconut oil)
    per half a squash
1 tsp pure maple syrup per half a squash
¼–½ tsp cinnamon sprinkled
Salt to taste
Chopped pecans

For the Chicken:

16 oz organic ground chicken
1–2 tbsps extra virgin olive oil
    (or coconut oil)

1 red onion, finely chopped
2–3 garlic bulbs, minced
3 cups organic spinach
½ tsp turmeric
2 tsps cumin
2 tsps coriander
½ tsp cinnamon
Salt and pepper to taste

Preheat the oven to 365°F.

Cut the squash in half and remove the seeds. Place in a baking pan and add the butter, maple syrup, cinnamon, and salt to taste. Make sure to spread the butter all around the squash in order for the flavor to seep in. Place in the oven and set the timer for 25 minutes.

In the meantime, pour the olive oil in a skillet and heat it over medium flame. Finely chop the garlic and onions and add them to the pan with the spinach. Cook until the onions are translucent and fragrant (about 2 minutes).

Add the ground chicken and chop it with a spatula. Sprinkle in the spices and mix everything around. Cook the chicken fully through and place it aside.

After 25 minutes, pull the rack with the squash out of the oven. Add the ground chicken mix and chopped pecans to each squash and place it back in the oven for another 15–20 minutes (or until the squash are soft).

Enjoy with other low carb sides, such as beets or cabbage.

Guide: GF, DF (with coconut oil), AI (with coconut oil), P

FROM SCRATCH SPANISH RICE AND BEANS

Makes 2 servings

When I returned from a trip to Costa Rica, I went on a rice and beans kick after having consumed these foods in some fashion every day for a couple of weeks. I loved the purity of Costa Rican food and how well it digested. Unlike many foods in the United States, there was very little processing involved in most of their dishes.

I became convinced I needed to avoid foods containing processed ingredients and brought this concept to my kitchen. From Scratch Spanish Rice and Beans became one of my regular dishes for the course of that entire month. It is a wonderful opportunity to enjoy a taste of Central America and food purity!

¾ cup black beans (dry measure)

1 tsp apple cider vinegar

3 cups + 3 cups + 1 cup filtered water

½ cup sprouted brown rice (dry measure)

2 garlic cloves, minced

2 tsps cumin

½ tsp oregano

½–1 tsp chili powder

1 whole organic red pepper, sliced

½ cup organic tomato sauce

1–2 tbsps coconut oil

Salt and Pepper to taste

Cilantro (optional for the topping)

Soak the beans in 3 cups of water with a tsp of apple cider vinegar for about 12 hours.

After this time has elapsed, drain and rinse the beans. Bring about 3 cups of water to a boil.

Cook the beans for 2 hours.

In a separate pot, bring one cup of water to a boil. Pour the rice into the pot, decrease the heat to low, and cover. Cook for about 25–30 minutes.

Note: Check the rice at 15–20 minutes, as it may soak up the water faster than the allotted time and may require more. Once done, place the rice aside.

On a cutting board, set up the pepper and the garlic. Cut the pepper in half, deseed, and slice it lengthwise. Next, peel, crush and mince the garlic.

In a medium skillet, heat the coconut oil over a medium flame. Add the onions, pepper, and minced garlic, along with the spices, and cook until the onions are translucent and the garlic is fragrant (about 3–5 minutes).

Add the tomato sauce. Allow it to marinate and simmer for about 2 minutes.

Add the cooked rice and beans to the skillet and mix everything until it is incorporated.

Transfer to a bowl or plate and garnish with cilantro leaves.

Guide: GF, DF, V

Calories: 586; Total Fat: 16.7 g; Sat Fat: 12.4 g; Cholesterol: 0 mg; Sodium: 352 mg; Total Carbohydrates: 71.3 g; Dietary Fiber: 15.1 g; Total Sugars: 10 g; Protein: 21.8g; Vitamin D: 0 mcg; Calcium: 148 mg; Iron: 7 mg; Potassium: 1647 mg

SOUPS

CREAMY SALMON, BUTTERNUT SQUASH, AND PEA SOUP

Makes 4 servings

This recipe was part of my gluten, dairy, egg, soy-free diet, Candida cleanse, and weight gain journey. I wanted to make a creamy dish to help decrease inflammation, pack in several nutrients, and target the Candida.

Challenging? Yes—but I was up for it. According to Traditional Chinese Medicine, Candida is caused by "dampness." Peas, vegetables, sprouted grains, beets, carrots, and rutabaga are considered beneficial, while starchy squash, yams, and potatoes are used sparingly. According to a typical anti-Candida diet, both coconut oil and bone broth are encouraged, as they help to eliminate the infection. Fish helps counter the inflammation. In terms of texture and taste, I was looking for creamy and savory. I believe I succeeded with this dish. When I first tasted it, I thought I had ordered something from a high-end restaurant. Dietary restrictions or not, this dish may be enjoyed by everyone!

2 tbsps coconut oil
12 oz salmon
1 can organic green peas

2 ½ cups butternut squash, cubed
½ cup full-fat coconut milk
½ cup organic bone broth
8 sprigs of fresh thyme (about 1 tbsp)
Salt and pepper to taste

In a 4-quart pot, heat the coconut oil over a medium flame. Add the butternut squash, salt, pepper, and fresh thyme. Toss the ingredients around and let it cook for 3–4 minutes.

Add in the bone broth until the butternut squash is almost covered. Increase the heat to a high flame. Once the liquid is boiling, turn the heat down to a low flame, keeping it at a simmer. Cook for 15 minutes or until the squash is almost soft.

In the meantime, chop the salmon into small pieces. At 15 minutes, add the salmon and peas and cook for another 5–10 minutes while keeping the liquid at a simmer.

Add in the coconut milk, stir until it is incorporated, and cook until warm.

Serve in a handled bowl with a soup spoon.

Guide: GF, DF, AI, P

Note: Make this dish low-GL (glycemic load) friendly by swapping the butternut squash for turnips or rutabaga.

> **Nutrition Facts (1 serving)**
>
> Calories: 441; Total Fat: 26.1 g; Sat Fat: 10.9 g; Cholesterol: 45 mg; Sodium: 248.2 mg; Total Carbohydrates: 29.1 g; Dietary Fiber: 7.6 g; Total Sugars: 10.5 g; Protein: 26.4 g; Vitamin D: 0 mcg; Calcium: 55 mg; Iron: 1.6 mg; Potassium: 311.9 mg

BEET, CARROT AND SWEET POTATO SOUP

Makes 3 servings

This dish is simple to put together, full of nutrition, and absolutely delicious. When I was on a diet that involved more warming and soft foods, I wanted to include something that would be good for my stomach while delivering several antioxidants to my system. At the time, I was also steering away from onions and garlic, which can be difficult when attempting to create a delicious soup recipe.

I find that, when I am stressed, simple, nutrient-dense foods are the answer. For this Beet Carrot and Sweet Potato Soup recipe, I added some thyme for extra flavor and for the additional health benefits. Not only is this spice excellent for digestion, I recently found out that it is a source of phytoestrogens—meaning, it may beneficial for those who need an estrogen boost.

2 tbsps extra virgin olive oil (sometimes referred to as EVOO)

1 tsp dried thyme

3 cups organic bone broth

¾ cup organic beets, cubed

1 cup organic baby carrots, diced

5 oz (or ¾ cup) sweet potato, cubed

Salt and pepper to taste

In a Dutch oven or 4-quart pot, heat the olive oil over medium heat. Add the cubed beets, baby carrots, sweet potato, salt, pepper, and thyme. Toss it all together and let it cook for about 2–4 minutes. This helps the flavor of the soup become more robust.

Add the broth until all of the vegetables are covered and bring to a boil. Turn down the heat and let it simmer until the vegetables are soft (about 25–30 minutes).

Remove it from the heat. With an immersion blender, puree the soup until everything is fully incorporated.

Guide: GF, DF, AI, P

Note #1: Want to add an extra source of protein? Try topping with pumpkin seeds or adding white beans.

Note #2: For extra flavor, first roast the sweet potato before adding it in and pureeing.

> **Nutrition Facts (1 serving)**
>
> Calories: 216; Total Fat: 9.9 g; Sat Fat: 1.3 g; Cholesterol: 10 mg; Sodium: 423.4 mg; Total Carbohydrates: 20.2 g; Dietary Fiber: 3.5 g; Total Sugars: 10.8 g; Protein: 11.2 g; Vitamin D: 0 mcg; Calcium: 86 mg; Iron: 1.9 mg; Potassium: 493 mg

CARROT GINGER SOUP

Makes 2–3 servings

There are nights when I crave something that is satisfying, rich in nutrients, and simple enough to prevent me from grabbing a "convenience" food.

This soup came to me because one of my all-time favorite juices is beet, carrot, ginger, and lemon juice. On a cold night, I thought, why not use two of these ingredients and turn it into a soup?

The combination of ingredients offers myriad nutritional benefits: the carrots keep your eyes, hair, skin and nails healthy; the ginger is a great antimicrobial and digestive aid; and the onions and garlic contain prebiotic fibers to help feed beneficial bacteria in your gut. It is truly a big win for a busy and freezing winter night!

1 bag organic baby carrots

1 large onion, chopped

2 garlic cloves, grated

1 thumb fresh ginger, grated

2–4 cups organic bone broth (vegetable broth for vegan)

Salt and pepper to taste

2 tbsps extra virgin olive oil

Peel and chop the onion. Place it aside.

Crush the garlic and let it sit for 5 minutes. Grate a thumb of ginger. Place all of these aside.

Add 2 tbsps of olive oil to the pot and place on medium heat.

Add the onion and let it sit until it turns almost pale. Add the garlic and ginger until they become fragrant (about 2 minutes).

Add the baby carrots and toss with the other ingredients. Add the salt, pepper, and broth to the pot.

Increase the heat to high until it boils. Reduce the heat down to low. Cook for an additional 45 minutes or until the carrots are tender.

Once the carrots are soft, blend all ingredients together with an immersion blender.

Note #1: For added protein, you can serve with chicken.

Note #2: Greens are also a great addition to this. Add some steamed kale to soup and top with pumpkin seeds for extra magnesium!

Guide: GF, DF, AI, V (with vegetable broth), P

Note #3: You can make a big batch of this and freeze it for quick access later on.

Nutrition Facts (1 serving)

Calories: 200; Total Fat: 9.6 g, Sat Fat: 1.4 g; Cholesterol: 0 mg; Sodium: 240 mg; Total Carbohydrates: 17.1 g; Dietary Fiber: 5.2 g; Total Sugars: 8.9 g; Protein: 13.6 g; Vitamin D: 0 mcg; Calcium: 61 mg; Iron: 1 mg; Potassium: 419 mg

---

SIDE DISHES

CURRIED SWEET POTATOES AND BUTTERNUT SQUASH

Makes 6 servings

One Fall day, I was asked to make a potato dish for a church event. Normally, a potato salad would come to mind but, since I am in love with curry spices, I decided to combine all of these ideas and go with sweet potatoes instead.

As I'm sure you've learned by now, I am fond of creating unique dishes that are packed with nutrition. The main ingredient in Curried Sweet Potatoes and Butternut Squash is turmeric, which has been identified as a potent cancer-fighting compound that is excellent for antioxidant status (due to the curcuminoids), as well as for improving brain health. The sweet potatoes and butternut squash are great sources of potassium, vitamin A, and vitamin B6, which make this dish not only warming, but also beneficial for heart health; healthy hair, skin, and nails; decreasing inflammation; and possibly even elevating mood.

4 cups sweet potatoes, cubed

2 cups butternut squash, cubed

2 tbsps coconut oil

1 tsp turmeric

1 tsp cinnamon

½ tsp coriander

½ tsp cumin

¼ tsp nutmeg

½ tsp sea salt

½ tsp ground black pepper

½ cup bone broth (vegetable broth
   for vegan)

Preheat the oven to 400°F.

On a cutting board, chop the butternut squash and sweet potatoes. Place them in a shallow casserole dish with the coconut oil, spices, salt, and pepper.

Toss the ingredients and transfer them to the oven. Cook until tender (about 45 minutes).

Remove from the oven and serve as a delicious side dish with a protein or bean meal.

Guide: GF, DF, AI, V (with vegetable broth), P

Nutrition Facts (1 serving)

Calories: 186; Total Fat: 5 g; Sat Fat: 4.1 g; Cholesterol: 0 mg; Sodium: 175 mg; Total Carbohydrates: 34.1 g; Dietary Fiber: 5.4 g; Total Sugars: 1.6 g; Protein: 2.9 g; Vitamin D: 0 mcg; Calcium: 56 mg; Iron: 1 mg; Potassium: 997 mg

HERBY BROCCOLI RABE CAULIFLOWER RICE

Makes 3–4 servings

A few years ago, I began to substitute cauliflower in place of grains and potatoes. The taste is not overpowering, plus it cooks much faster than normal rice.

One day, while I was at the local grocery store, I noticed that the broccoli rabe was on sale and thought it was time for me to switch things up.

Broccoli rabe is a wonderful bitter green to pair with proteins. It is a cruciferous vegetable, which means it is excellent for liver detox. It actually packs a double punch when paired with the cauliflower—yet another cruciferous vegetable!

I had wanted some variety and this recipe fit the bill. My family is into Penzeys Spices—a Wisconsin-based retail, catalog, and mail order company that distributes quality spices—so we love playing around with all the samples we receive when our orders arrive.

3 cups riced cauliflower
1 head of organic broccoli rabe, chopped
2 cloves garlic, minced
½ tsp fresh thyme
½ tsp fresh sage
½ tsp fresh rosemary
Salt and pepper to taste
1–2 tbsps coconut oil

Rinse and chop the cauliflower into small sprouts. Drop them into a food processor and blend until a rice is formed. Place this aside. Note do not over-process, or else it will come out too fine and not have a rice consistency.

In a skillet, heat the coconut oil over a medium flame. Add the broccoli rabe and cook for about 2 minutes. Add the rest of the ingredients and mix until everything is incorporated. Cook until the rice is tender (about 3–5 minutes).

Guide: GF, DF, AI, V, P

Nutrition Facts (1 serving)

Calories: 105; Total Fat: 4.5 g; Sat Fat: 3 g; Cholesterol: 0 mg; Sodium: 146 mg; Total Carbohydrates: 10.9 g; Dietary Fiber: 7.7 g; Total Sugars: 2.4 g; Protein: 8.7 g; Vitamin D: 0 mcg; Calcium: 266 mg; Iron: 5 mg; Potassium: 450 mg

RUTABAGA AND CARROT MASH

Makes 4 servings

This is an excellent side dish for those people who are trying to avoid nightshades or are incorporating more low glycemic sources into their diets.

This Rutabaga and Carrot Mash recipe originated during a time in which my liver needed a little support. I could only consume limited ingredient dishes and I was mostly on a pureed food diet. Rutabaga is low in carbohydrates but, as a cruciferous vegetable, it can also assist with phase 2 liver detox, which helps rid the body of harmful detoxification products from phase 1 liver detox. Since the vegetable is also slightly sweet, I decided to add in some carrot to the mix to compliment the flavor.

This dish was a hit right from the get-go with my family. It's another delicious and nutritious recipe that is quick and easy to prepare.

2–3 cups of water, for steaming
2 cups rutabaga, cubed
2 large carrots, chopped
1 tbsp coconut oil
Salt and pepper to taste

Peel and chop the carrots and rutabaga on a cutting board.

In a steamer, bring the water to a boil. Add the carrots and rutabaga and then cover. After about 5 minutes, turn the heat down to a medium-high flame. Cook for another 15–20 minutes or until tender.

When it's ready, transfer the mix into a large bowl. With a fork or potato masher, process the carrots and rutabaga until they are fully incorporated. They should resemble the consistency of mashed potatoes.

Add the coconut oil, salt, and pepper. Mix well.

Guide: GF, DF, AI, V, P

Nutrition Facts (1 serving)

Calories: 62; Total Fat: 3.6 g; Sat Fat: 3 g; Cholesterol: 0 mg; Sodium: 100.1 mg; Total Carbohydrates: 6.8 g; Dietary Fiber: 2.3 g; Sugars: 3.7 g; Protein: 1 g; Vitamin D: 0 mcg; Calcium: 63 mg; Iron: .3 mg; Potassium: 115 mg

---

SWEETENED CAULIFLOWER RICE

Makes 3 servings

One of my favorite books for nutritional guidance is Paul Pitchford's Healing with Whole Foods. I happened to be reading a passage about a spleen qi diet and warming foods that could help circulate the blood and, possibly, ease stress. One of the recipes Pitchford recommends is this sweetened rice, which uses warming medicinal spices, such as turmeric and cinnamon, and adds in a little cumin to help the pancreas to release digestive enzymes.

At this point, while I was staying away from grains, I continued to desire that delicious warming taste, so I decided to sub in the cauliflower. Cauliflower adds in a great nutritional punch; it is a source of indole-3-carbinol, which converts to a compound called DIM (diindolylmethane), which aids in the clearance of estrogen in the body. Not only is this warming to the body, it also helps you relax from all of its terrific flavors. It was even a hit with my mom, who usually does not eat sweet potatoes.

3 ½ cups riced cauliflower

1 cup sweet potatoes, cubed in ½ inch pieces

3 tbsps organic raisins

1 ½ tbsps coconut oil

⅛ tsp turmeric

⅛ tsp cinnamon

⅛ tsp cumin

⅛ tsp coriander

⅛ tsp ginger

Chop and rice the cauliflower in a food processor. Do not over process or it will come out slightly mushy.

Place chopped sweet potatoes in the steamer and bring to a boil. Turn heat to medium high flame and cook until tender, about 5 minutes. (Note: The smaller you cube the sweet potatoes the less time they will take to cook).

In the meantime, heat the coconut oil in a skillet over medium high flame. Once melted, add the cauliflower, spices, and raisins and toss until incorporated. Cook for about 2 minutes before adding the steamed sweet potatoes and toss until incorporated. Cook for another 2 minutes for the flavors to seep in.

Guide: GF, DF, AI, V, P

Nutrition Facts (1 serving)

Calories: 176; Total Fat: 7 g; Sat Fat: 5.9 g; Cholesterol: 0 mg; Sodium: 101 mg; Total Carbohydrates: 26.4 g; Dietary Fiber: 4.5 g; Total Sugars: 7.6 g; Protein: 3.1 g; Vitamin D: 0 mcg; Calcium: 35 mg; Iron: 1 mg; Potassium: 481 mg

WARMING HERB ARUGULA AND BUTTERNUT SQUASH

Makes 2 servings

Early one summer, I discovered a recipe incorporating sage, thyme, and rosemary, which I happened to be growing in my yard. By Fall, the herbs were still flourishing, and I wanted to put them to good use before it was too late. I uncovered this recipe and added a few twists, including playing around with different oils. Ultimately, I decided to go with a lighter flavor, such as coconut oil.

Sage and thyme, in particular, are excellent for fighting cancer and are also sources of phytoestrogens—which may be beneficial for those experiencing menopause and/or seeking to detox excess estrogen.

In the end, I realized I had created a delicious dish that has bittersweet undertones and is a rich source of nutrients.

1 cup butternut squash, cubed
2–3 cups organic arugula
1 tbsp coconut oil
1 tsp fresh thyme
1 tsp fresh sage
1 tsp fresh rosemary
Salt and pepper to taste

Place the butternut squash in a steamer and cook until it's almost soft (about 10 minutes). Place it aside.

Heat the oil over a medium flame. Add the arugula, salt, pepper, and herbs. Cook until the arugula is almost wilted (about 4 minutes). Add the butternut squash to the pan and toss. Cook for another 2–3 minutes until soft.

Guide: GF, DF, V, AI, P

Nutrition Facts (1 serving)

Calories: 103; Total Fat: 7.3 g; Sat Fat: 6 g; Cholesterol: 0 mg; Sodium: 13 mg; Total Carbohydrates: 10.4 g; Dietary Fiber: 2.7 g; Total Sugars: 1.6 g; Protein: 1.6 g; Vitamin D: 0 mcg; Calcium: 106 mg; Iron: 2 mg; Potassium: 260 mg

---

ROSEMARY THYME MASHED POTATOES

Makes 3 servings

During the summers, I enjoy growing herbs in my backyard and incorporating them into my recipes. Not only are they tasty, but they pack a mean micronutrient punch. I especially like combining my homegrown herbs with potatoes, which is why I created this side dish. Potatoes are a strong source of potassium and also contain essential nutrients, such as chromium for insulin sensitivity, and vitamin B6 for boosting mood.

10 organic baby red potatoes

4 cups filtered water

2 tbsps extra virgin olive oil

2 tsps fresh thyme leaves

2 tbsps fresh rosemary leaves

Pinch of garlic powder

Salt and pepper to taste

Rinse and add 10 organic baby red potatoes to a medium pot. Fill up the pot with 4 cups of filtered water or until the potatoes are fully submerged.

Place the potatoes over high heat and boil them for about 30 minutes.

Note: You also have the option of cutting up the potatoes and steaming them instead of boiling them.

Drain the potatoes and place them in a large stainless-steel bowl. With a potato masher, start to mash the potatoes so they are spread out in the bowl.

Add the rest of the ingredients to the potatoes and continue to mash until they are smooth.

Guide: GF, DF, V

Nutritional Facts (1 serving)

Calories: 164; Total Fat: 9.1 g; Sat Fat: 1.3 g; Cholesterol: 0 mg; Sodium: 32.4 mg; Total Carbohydrates: 18.6 g; Dietary Fiber: 1.8 g; Total Sugars: 1.3 g; Protein: 2.4 g; Vitamin D: 0 mcg; Calcium: 88 mg; Iron: 1 mg; Potassium: 519 mg

DESSERTS

PALEO(ISH) CARROT CAKE CUPCAKES

Makes 12 cupcakes

Hands down, carrot cake is one of my favorite desserts. It reminds me of when I was young, and my mom brought me to the café near where she worked to pick up a carrot cake for the week. Of course, she gave me a taste!

My quest of late has been to bring back this much-loved treat in a healthier fashion, so that I could relive my childhood as well as reap the nutritional benefits of the dish. I experimented with a few different paleo recipes and fused together the parts I liked.

The eggs and fat add density to my Paleo(ish) Carrot Cake Cupcakes, while the almond flour offers extra fiber and healthy fats. These cupcakes have become such a hit that my mom even requested them this past year for her birthday!

The recipe below includes a slight twist: The frosting is not your typical frosting, as it's dairy-free. I found this wonderful recipe from the Cotter Crunch blog https://www.cottercrunch.com. Of course, I tweaked and spiced it up to complete the perfect topping for this delicious classic.

For the Cake:

5 large organic carrots, grated

2 tbsps pure maple syrup

1 cup almond flour

¾ cup arrowroot flour

1 tsp baking soda

1 tsp aluminum-free baking powder

2 ½ tsps cinnamon

½ tsp nutmeg

1 tsp sea salt

½ cup (1 stick) grass-fed butter

3 organic, pasture-raised eggs

½ cup organic brown sugar *or* coconut sugar

1 tsp vanilla extract (or ½ tsp double-strength vanilla extract)

½ cup organic raisins

For the Frosting:

1 can coconut cream

1 tbsp pure maple syrup

½ tsp vanilla extract

For the Cupcakes:

Preheat the oven to 350°F.

Peel the carrots and process them in a food processor. Transfer them to a Pyrex container and drizzle the maple syrup. Place them in the refrigerator and allow them to marinate.

In a large bowl, add and mix all of the dry ingredients—aside from the sugar—until they are incorporated.

Heat the butter in the microwave or over the stove until it is fully melted. Let it cool slightly (about 5 minutes).

In a smaller bowl, add the eggs, melted butter, vanilla extract, and brown sugar. With a hand mixer, beat the ingredients until they are incorporated.

Pour half of the wet mixture into the bowl with the dry ingredients and beat them together with a hand mixer on medium speed. Once incorporated, add in the rest of the wet ingredients while continuing to mix.

Fold in the raisins with a spatula until they are fully incorporated.

Place baking cups in a muffin tin. Fill each with ¼ cup portions of the cupcake mix.

Place the muffin tin in the oven about 25–30 minutes. Insert and remove a toothpick into each cupcake to ensure it is fully cooked and comes out clean.

Remove from the oven and let it sit for about 5 minutes. Transfer to a cooling rack and start to whip up the frosting.

For the Frosting:

Cool the coconut cream overnight in the refrigerator.

Separate the solid from the liquid and transfer to a chilled stainless-steel bowl. Whip with a hand mixer until peaks start to form. Add the maple syrup and vanilla and continue to whip until peaks are fully formed.

Place the coconut cream frosting in a piping bag and frost your cupcakes.

Guide: GF, P (with coconut sugar)

Nutrition Facts (1 serving)

Calories: 350; Total Fat: 23 g; Sat Fat: 15.2 g; Cholesterol: 66.3 mg; Sodium: 355.5 mg; Total Carbohydrates: 31.5 g; Dietary Fiber: 2.5 g; Sugars: 15.6 g; Protein: 4.1 g; Vitamin D: 0 mcg; Calcium: 125 mg; Iron: .8 mg; Potassium: 216.6 mg

"TWO-YEAR-OLD APPROVED"
VEGAN CARROT CAKE CUPCAKE

Makes 10 servings

In 2018, we discovered that my nephew had dairy allergy, which meant cutting a lot of staples out of his diet. Unfortunately, cake was one of the forbidden foods.

For his second birthday, I became determined to make a special cake that he could enjoy. I stumbled across a gluten-free vegan vanilla cupcake recipe on the lovingitvegan blog at https://lovingit-vegan.com. At around the same time, I found a standard carrot cake recipe in one of my cookbooks.

I decided to combine aspects of both recipes and add my own twists. Not only did my nephew like the result, it became a hit among everyone seated at the table. I am, therefore, pleased to present to you egg-free, gluten-free, dairy-free cupcakes that are truly marvelous for any celebration—and people of any age.

1 cup organic, gluten-free rolled oats, made into a flour
¾ cup gluten-free all-purpose flour
2 tbsps organic sugar
1 tsp baking soda
½ tsp sea salt
1 tsp cinnamon
½ tsp nutmeg
⅛ tsp cloves
1 cup unsweetened coconut milk
10 organic baby carrots, grated
10 Medjool dates, made into a paste
½ cup coconut oil, melted
1 tbsp apple cider vinegar
1 toothpick
Top With: Coconut Cream Frosting (located in the Paleo(ish) Carrot Cake Cupcake recipe)

Preheat the oven to 350°F.

Grate 10 baby carrots in a food processor and set them aside.

Place the oats in blender and process them into a flour.

Place 10 dates in a bowl with 2–4 tbsps of water. Place in a microwave for 25 seconds. Use a fork to mash them into a paste.

Sift together the gluten-free flour and oat flour into a large bowl. Add the rest of the dry ingredients and mix them together.

In a smaller bowl, add all of the wet ingredients and beat them together until they are incorporated.

Add the wet ingredients to the dry ingredients and beat them together until they are incorporated.

Add the grated carrots and fold them in with a spatula.

Line a muffin tin with baking cups and use ¼ cup measure to fill them.

Place in the oven for 25 minutes. Insert and remove a toothpick into a cupcake to ensure it is fully cooked and comes out clean.

Top each cupcake with coconut cream frosting from the Paleo(ish) Carrot Cake Cupcakes

Guide: DF, GF, V

Nutrition Facts (1 serving)

Calories: 369; Total Fat: 24.5 g; Sat Fat: 21.7 g; Cholesterol: 0 mg; Sodium: 133.9 mg; Total Carbohydrates: 35.5 g; Dietary Fiber: 4.1 g; Total Sugars: 17.2 g; Protein: 3.3 g; Vitamin D: 0 mcg; Calcium: 61 mg; Iron: 1.1 mg; Potassium: 198 mg

HEALTHY STRAWBERRY SHORTCAKES

Makes about 12 mini shortcakes

I love when my church has bake sales. It gives me a chance to experiment with new recipes, as well as throw in my healthy, gluten-free kick.

After having prepared so many desserts for so many bake sales, I racked my brain to come up with something new for an event. Since it was June, I came up with the idea of using strawberries in one of my recipes. I searched high and low for an appropriate cupcakes recipe and stumbled on one from lovingit-vegan's blog at https://lovingitvegan.com.

As usual, I put my own spin on the recipe by using dates and oat flour, which provide fiber and slow digesting carbohydrates and antioxidants. (I try to get highest possible nutrient density in a dish as I can!)

This summer treat became a huge hit among the consumers at the bake sale. Without further adieu: Healthy Strawberry Shortcakes.

For the Cupcakes:

- 1 cup gluten free oats, made into a flour
- ¾ cup gluten-free all-purpose flour
- 16 Medjool dates, pitted and made into a paste
- 1 tsp baking soda
- ½ tsp pink Himalayan sea salt
- 1 tsp vanilla extract
- ⅛ cup coconut oil, melted
- ½ cup full-fat coconut milk
- ½ cup water
- 1 tbsp apple cider vinegar
- 2 tbsps organic apple sauce
- 1 toothpick

For the Frosting:

- 1 13.5 oz can coconut cream, solid only
- 3 tbsps pure maple syrup
- ½ tsp vanilla extract
- Top with:1 cup sliced strawberries (divided)

For the Cupcakes:

Preheat the oven to 350°F.

Place 1 cup of oats in a food processor and blend them into a flour.

Sift the oat flour and gluten-free flour together in a medium sized bowl and add the rest of the dry ingredients. Place the bowl aside.

In a large bowl, combine all of the wet ingredients and blend them with a hand mixer until they are incorporated.

Add the dry ingredients to the wet ingredients while slowly continuing to whisk. Set this aside.

Line a muffin tin with baking cups. With ¼ measuring cup, pour the batter evenly amongst the 12 baking cups.

Place in the oven and bake for about 25 minutes. Insert and remove a toothpick into a cupcake to ensure it is fully cooked and comes out clean.

Transfer to a cooling rack.

For the Frosting:

Chill 1 13.5 oz can of coconut cream in the refrigerator overnight. The next day, separate solid white cream at the top, leaving behind the liquid, and scoop it into a large bowl. With a hand mixer, process until fluffy and whipped.

Add in the vanilla while continuing to mix. Pour in the maple syrup 1 tbsp at a time. Place it aside.

When the cupcakes have cooled, cut them through the middle to create a sandwich.

Frost the middle and the top. Crown each layer with 2–3 sliced strawberries.

Note: You do not want to add too many strawberries or the cupcake will keel over!

Guide: GF, DF, V

Nutrition Facts (recipe alone)
(1 serving)

Calories: 278 calories; Total Fat: 13.1 g; Sat Fat: 11.4 g; Cholesterol: 0 mg; Sodium: 180 mg; Total Carbohydrates: 38 g; Dietary Fiber: 3.3 g; Sugars: 20.9 g; Protein: 2.9 g; Vitamin D: 0 mcg; Calcium: 26 mg; Iron: .8 mg; Potassium: 120.4 mg

APPLE, OAT, AND A LITTLE SPICE CUPCAKES WITH COCONUT CREAM FROSTING

One day I challenged myself in the kitchen by attempting to create a gluten-free, dairy-free, vegan version of a fall flavored cupcake with apple spice.

I always prefer to use whole food sources rather than processed vegan butters. In the past, I had made whipped cream with coconut cream, so I thought it would be a wonderful ingredient to use as part of the frosting.

These cupcakes are not only scrumptious, they contain some loving ingredients that your body will be thanking you for. These are sweetened with dates, which adds an extra source of fiber and nutrients, such as potassium, calcium, and magnesium; these are beneficial for bone health and blood sugar regulation. When you are searching for a healthy recipe for a bake sale, these cupcakes are an excellent go-to!

For the Cupcakes:

1 cup gluten-free oats, made into a flour
¾ cups gluten-free all-purpose flour
10 Medjool dates, made into a paste
2 tbsps coconut sugar
1 tsp baking soda

1 tsp cinnamon
¼ tsp salt
1 cup non-dairy milk
1 organic apple, peeled and finely chopped
1 tsp vanilla extract
1 tbsp organic apple cider vinegar
1 toothpick

For the Topping:

1 can full-fat coconut creme
1 tsp cinnamon
1 tbsp pure maple syrup or raw honey

For the Cupcakes:

Preheat the oven to 350°F.

In a blender, grind the oats down to a flour. Add all of the dry ingredients and pulse until they have become sifted.

Transfer to a medium sized bowl.

In a larger bowl, combine all of the wet ingredients and blend them with a hand mixer on low until they are incorporated.

Continue mixing, slowly combining the dry ingredients with the wet ingredients.

Once incorporated, add in the apple with a spatula.

Line a muffin tin with baking cups and fill each ¾ of the way.

Bake for 25 minutes. Insert and remove a toothpick into a cupcake to ensure it is fully cooked and comes out clean.

For the Frosting:

Refrigerate the coconut creme overnight. Drain the liquid and scoop out the pulp into a medium sized bowl. With a hand mixer, process the coconut until it becomes creamy.

Add the raw honey and vanilla extract.

Continue to mix with a hand mixer until peaks form (about 1 minute).

Add the cream to a frosting bag and top the cupcakes.

Add extra cinnamon for garnish.

Guide: GF, DF, V

Nutrition Facts (1 serving)

Calories: 238; Total Fat: 11.4 g; Sat Fat: 10.1 g; Cholesterol: 0 mg; Sodium: 153.5 mg; Total Carbohydrates: 34.6 g; Dietary Fiber: 4.6 g; Total Sugars: 18.2 g; Protein: 2.6 g; Vitamin D: 0 mcg; Calcium: 74 mg; Iron: .8 mg; Potassium: 254.9 mg

CHOCOLATE IS FOR GUT LOVERS CUPCAKES

Makes 12 servings

After having created several gluten-free, dairy free, and vegan recipes, I wanted to tap into my chocolate cravings and create a healthy alternative to the typical chocolate cupcake. It all started when I stumbled on a recipe for Gluten-Free Vegan Matcha Cupcakes on the lovingitvegan blog at https:// lovingitvegan.com. The recipes on this site are amazing and, since I discovered them, I have been concocting some pretty amazing flavor combinations with extra nutritional benefits.

Chocolate Is for Gut Lovers Cupcakes is made with coconut oil—an excellent source of caprylic acid, which helps fight off harmful bacteria. The oats and raw honey provide prebiotic fibers that help feed and repopulate beneficial gut bacteria. Raw honey is particularly high in oligosaccharides, which have been shown to increase immune-boosting Bifidobacter spp. The coconut sugar is an unrefined alternative that is high in B vitamins to improve protein, carbohydrate, and fat digestion.

Fully delicious and fully functional: This is how I roll when I bake for an event!

For the Cupcakes:

1 cup gluten-free oats, made into a flour
¾ cup gluten-free all-purpose flour
1 cup organic coconut sugar
1 tsp baking soda
½ cup organic cocoa powder
1 cup non-dairy milk
⅓ cup organic unrefined coconut oil
1 tsp vanilla extract
1 tbsp organic raw apple cider vinegar
¼ tsp pink Himalayan sea salt
1 toothpick

For the Frosting:

1 can coconut cream
3 tbsps strawberry puree
1 tbsp raw honey

For the Cupcakes:

Preheat the oven to 350°F.

Place the gluten-free rolled oats in a blender and process into a flour. Add the gluten-free flour, baking soda, salt, and cocoa powder in the blender and combine until the ingredients are fully sifted. Transfer the contents to a large bowl and whisk in the coconut sugar.

In a medium-sized bowl, combine the non-dairy milk, melted coconut oil, and vanilla extract using a handheld mixer.

Combine the wet ingredients with the dry ingredients. Mix until everything is incorporated.

Line a muffin tray with 12 baking cups and fill each up with about a ¼ cup serving.

Place in the oven for about 25 minutes. Insert and remove a toothpick into a cupcake to ensure it is fully cooked and comes out clean.

Transfer to a cooling rack and allow to sit until cool (about 10 minutes).

For the Frosting:

Place one can of coconut cream upside down in the refrigerator overnight.

Drain the liquid in a small bowl and scoop out the solid portion into a large bowl. Mix with a hand mixer until peaks start to form.

Add in the strawberry puree and raw honey and mix until the cream is smooth.

Transfer to a frosting bag and top the cupcakes. Serve immediately or place in the refrigerator.

Guide: GF, DF, V

Nutrition Facts (1 serving)

Calories: 250; Total Fat: 14.8 g; Sat Fat: 12.1 g; Cholesterol: 0 mg; Sodium: 142 mg; Total Carbohydrates: 26.4 g; Dietary Fiber: 5.3 g; Total Sugars: 15 g; Protein: 3.4 g; Vitamin D: 0 mcg; Calcium: 42 mg; Iron: 2 mg; Potassium: 461 mg

RECOVERY YAM BROWNIES

Makes 16 Servings

When I created Recovery Yam Brownies, I was looking for different ingredients that would replace unhealthy regular brownies while also helping with muscle recovery from exercise. I am an avid cyclist, so I wanted to make something that was full of antioxidants, complex carbohydrates, and nutrient density for recovery after rides.

I read that beets help with faster delivery of nutrients to muscles and that cocoa helps with muscle recovery and cellular repair. Vitamin E can play a role in free radical scavenging after a long workout.

With these facts in mind, I sought to combine them all in a recipe. I had an idea in mind, but I admit that I had a little help from a friend (thank you, https://chocolatecoveredkatie.com blog!).

These delicious brownies are refined sugar free, high in fiber, and suitable as a healthy alternative to your typical brownie.

1 cup yams, pureed
1 cup gluten-free oats, made into a flour
¼ cup + ⅛ cup cocoa powder
1 ½ tsps baking soda

2 tsps beet root powder
⅛ tsp salt
½ cup coconut oil
2–3 tbsps for the date paste
6–8 Medjool dates, made into a paste
¼ cup sunflower butter
¼ cup non-dairy milk
1 toothpick

Pre-heat oven to 365°F.

Place the sweet potato into oven and bake until tender, about 45 to 60 minutes.

When it's done, take the yam out of the oven, remove the skin from and place in a small bowl.

With an immersion blender, process the yam until a puree is formed. Place aside.

Remove the pit from 6–8 dates and add to a saucepan with 2–3 tbsps of water. Place it on low-medium heat. Once steam starts to form, remove the dates from the heat.

Adjust the temperature of the oven to 350°F.

Measure one cup of oats transfer them to a blender, and process until a flour is formed.

In a medium-sized bowl, add all dry ingredients and stir until incorporated.

In a separate bowl, add the pureed yam along with the date paste, melted coconut oil, sunflower butter, and non-dairy milk of choice. Mix it all together using a hand mixer.

Slowly add the dry ingredients and mix until everything is fully incorporated.

Add the brownie mix to an oiled baking dish lined with parchment paper. Smooth the top and transfer to the oven.

Bake for about 20–30 minutes. Insert and remove a toothpick into the mix to ensure it is fully cooked and comes out clean.

Guide: GF, DF, V

Nutrition Facts (1 serving)

Calories: 138; Total Fat: 11 g; Sat Fat: 6.5 g; Cholesterol: 0 mg; Sodium: 160.5 mg; Total Carbohydrates: 10.3 g; Dietary Fiber: 2.4 g; Total Sugars: 2.9 g; Protein: 2.2 g; Vitamin D: 0 mcg; Calcium: 13.5 mg; Iron: .75 mg; Potassium: 144 mg

---

CHICKPEA BROWNIES

Makes 9 Brownies

Beans can be a great addition to any diet as a source of fiber, folate, and plant-based proteins, but they can also make an excellent foundation for decadent brownies.

I was inspired to come up with this idea from all of the black bean brownie recipes I had seen. Chickpeas have a little milder flavor, however, and, after using them as a base for cookies, I thought: Why not just make some brownies? (Actually, how about a brownie/cookie mix with chickpeas? You'll have to stay tuned for the next cookbook....)

Chickpea Brownies are a great source of phytoestrogens, which may help with menopausal symptoms. Couple that with the dopamine enhancing properties of chocolate and the cancer fighting compounds in the flax seed and you have a nourishing and decadent dish that will help keep your body functioning at an optimal level.

1 can chickpeas (keep the liquid)
2 flax eggs (1 tbsp flax to 3 tbsps water per flax egg)
⅔ cup raw cacao powder
⅓ cup organic extra virgin coconut oil

¼ cup pure maple syrup + 1 tbsp organic coconut sugar
1 tbsp baking soda
½ tsp extra strength vanilla (or 1 tsp vanilla extract)
2 tsps almond butter (optional)
1 toothpick

Preheat oven to 350°F. Spray 8 x 8 (20 x 20 cm) baking dish with coconut or extra virgin olive oil cooking spray. (You can butter to grease the pan instead.)

In a blender or food processor, place the beans, melted coconut oil, 1–2 tbsp liquid from the beans and ⅓ cup chocolate. Blend well.

Add flax eggs, cocoa, maple syrup, baking powder, and vanilla to the mixture and blend until smooth. Add almond butter, if desired, and pulse.

Bake for 20–25 minutes. Insert and remove a toothpick into the mix to ensure it is fully cooked and comes out clean. Store in a refrigerator.

Guide: GF, DF, V

> **Nutrition Facts (1 serving)**
>
> Calories: 180; Total Fat: 9.3 g; Sat Fat: 7.1 g; Cholesterol: 0 mg; Sodium: 62.3 mg; Total Carbohydrates: 18.7 g; Dietary Fiber: 5 g; Total Sugars: 5.7 g; Protein: 4.7 g; Vitamin D: 0 mcg; Calcium: 38 mg; Iron: 0 mg; Potassium: 165.5 mg

PUMPKIN CHOCOLATE CHIP COOKIES

Makes 12 cookies

Pumpkin and chocolate chip cookies are two of my favorite foods!

Unfortunately, when you are gluten-free, it is hard to enjoy these treats, so I became determined to find a grain-free alternative that would help replenish the body instead of deplete it—yet still be palatable.

I have to say, you can't go wrong anytime you add chocolate chips to a dessert. Cocoa is also beneficial to your central nervous system, due the presence of magnesium; it may even improve your mood, as it can help to increase dopamine levels.

Add in the pumpkin and you have an additional flavor kick and source of fiber, beta carotene (to provide antioxidant protection), and potassium (for blood sugar regulation and healthy fluid electrolyte balance).

Looking for a healthy alternative that will warm you emotionally? This is an excellent go-to!

1 cup almond flour
1 tbsp coconut flour
1 organic, pasture raised egg
1 tbsp organic unrefined extra virgin
   coconut oil

¼ cup pumpkin puree
3 tbsps raw honey
1 tsp vanilla extract
⅛ tsp pink Himalayan sea salt
¼ tsp baking soda
¼ tsp pumpkin pie spice
¼ cup (or more) dairy-free chocolate
   chips

Preheat oven to 350°F.

In a medium mixing bowl, sift the almond flour, coconut flour, baking soda, and salt.

Add in pumpkin puree, egg, raw honey, oil, and vanilla. Mix well.

Using a tablespoon measuring spoon, drop tablespoons of dough on sheet.

Bake for 15 minutes.

Guide: GF, DF, P

Nutrition Facts (1 serving)

Calories: 253; Total Fat: 15.5 g; Sat Fat: 6.8 g; Cholesterol: 74 mg; Sodium: 422.1 mg; Total Carbohydrates: 22.5 g; Dietary Fiber: 6.7 g; Total Sugars: 11.1 g; Protein: 7.2 g; Vitamin D: 0 mcg; Calcium: 61 mg; Iron: 3.3 mg; Potassium: 48.9 mg

SWEET TOOTH-SATISFYING ROASTED SWEET POTATOES AND PARSNIPS

Makes 3–4 servings

In case you haven't figured it out by now, I tend to have a bit of a sweet tooth. Cake, cookies, you name it!

I was once on a cleanse that was high in fruits and vegetables and low in sugars. I read in one of my nutritional healing books that sweet carbohydrate rich foods, such as parsnips and sweet potatoes, help to curb a sweet tooth. I wanted to put this to the test and decided to concoct a dessert dish that included some of my favorite sweet root vegetables.

With this dessert, you are not only curbing your sweet tooth, you are also replenishing your body with vital nutrients and antioxidants, instead of depleting your body of these elements with sugar. This has become a go-to for me even when I'm off the cleanse!

1 cup parsnips, chopped
1 cup sweet potato, cubed
2 tbsps coconut oil

¼ cup bone broth (just enough to coat the bottom) (vegetable broth for vegan)
1 tsp cinnamon
½ tsp nutmeg
Dash of pink Himalayan sea salt

Pre-heat the oven to 400°F.

Place the cubed sweet potatoes and parsnips in a large casserole dish. Toss them with the coconut oil, bone broth, and spices.

Slide the dish into the oven and bake until tender (about 45 minutes).

Remove from the oven and let it cool for about 5 minutes.

With an immersion blender, puree the sweet potato and the parsnips until they are fully incorporated.

Serve in a desert dish and top with 1 tbsp of your favorite nut or seed butter!

Guide: GF, DF, V (with vegetable broth), AI, P

Note: Allergic to nuts? Top with 1 tbsp organic sunflower seed butter or tahini mixed with ¼ tsp pure maple syrup!

Nutrition Facts (1 serving)

Recipe alone:

Calories: 128; Total Fat: 7.1 g; Sat Fat: 6 g; Cholesterol: 0 mg; Sodium: 43 mg; Total Carbohydrates: 15.9 g; Dietary Fiber: 3.3 g; Sugars: 1.9 g; Protein: 1.5 g; Vitamin D: 0 mcg; Calcium: 23 mg; Iron: 0 mg; Potassium: 356 mg

Add nut butter:

Calories: 227; Total Fat: 16.3 g; Sat Fat: 6 g; Cholesterol: 0 mg; Sodium: 113 mg; Total Carbohydrates: 19.3 g; Dietary Fiber: 3.9 g; Sugars: 2.6 g; Protein: 3.9 g; Vitamin D: 0 mcg; Calcium: 65 mg; Iron: 1 mg; Potassium: 474 mg

---

PEANUT BUTTER YUMS

Makes 12 Bites

When it comes to engaging with the kids, it is great to have recipes with a lot of ingredients. This give them the option to cater the recipe to their individual likes and makes it fun and simple. These fit the description and are a healthy alternative to several of the sugary snacks the kids tend to run for. Want to go nuts with the family? Make these fun peanut butter yums the next family project!

4 heaping tbsps organic peanut butter

2 tbsps coconut flakes + 2 tbsps for coating

2 tbsps chocolate chips

1–2 tbsps organic raisins

1 tbsp hemp seeds

3 tbsps gluten-free rolled oats

½ tbsp raw honey

¼ tsp cinnamon

Dash of ground cloves

Dash of vanilla extract

Place all ingredients in a large bowl, aside from the 2 extra tbsps of coconut flakes, and mix until fully incorporated.

Place the other 2 tbsps of coconut flakes in a separate bowl. Scoop out 1 heaping tbsp of batter with a measuring spoon and roll into 1 ½″ bites with your hands. Dip and roll each bite into the coconut flakes and transfer to a bowl.

Guide: GF, DF, V

Nutrition Facts (1 serving)

Calories: 93; Total Fat: 6.3 g; Sat Fat: 2.7 g; Cholesterol: 0 mg; Sodium: 0.4 mg; Total Carbohydrates: 5.9 g; Dietary Fiber: 1.3 g; Total Sugars: 3.5 g; Protein: 0.7 g; Vitamin D: 0 mcg; Calcium: 80 mg; Iron: 1 mg; Potassium: 42 mg

RECOMMENDED BRANDS AND PRODUCTS USED FOR THIS COOKBOOK

Note: Several different products were used in preparation of this cookbook. Here are some of my favorites, as well as information on where they can be purchased online. Brand names are indicated in *italics*.

Penzeys Spices

Bob's Red Mill: Coconut Flour, Toasted Carob Powder, Dried Beans, Lentils, Coconut Sugar, Golden Flaxseed Meal, Gluten-Free All-Purpose Flour, Arrowroot Flour

Brad's Organic: Almond Flour, Coconut Oil, Organic Tahini

Kara MD: Beetroot Powder (Recipe used in: Recovery Yam Brownies)

Kerry Gold: Irish Grass-Fed Butter

Let's Do Organic: Coconut Crème (Recipe used in: Apple, Oat and a Little Spice Cupcakes with Coconut Crème Frosting)

Navitas Organics: Cocoa Powder, Maca Powder (Recipes used in: Carob Cocoa Chia Pudding, Antioxidant Booster Smoothie, Happy Hormone Berry Smoothie), Chia Seeds (Recipes used in: Sweet Potato Crepes with Chocolate Overnight Oats, Straight from the Tropics Chia Pudding, Carob Cocoa Chia Pudding, Acai Chia Pudding, All Overnight Oat Recipes), Camu Camu Powder (Recipes used in: Antioxidant Punch Smoothie)

One Degree Organic: Gluten-Free Sprouted Rolled Oats, Gluten-Free Sprouted Steel Cut Oats

Pacific Brand: Organic Bone Broth

Sambazon: Organic Acai Packets (Recipe used in: Acai Bowl)

Sun Butter: Sunflower Seed Butter (Recipe used in: Recovery Yam Brownies)

The Real Coconut: Coconut Flour Tortillas (Recipe used in: Paleo Fiesta Fish Tacos)

Trader Joe's: Riced Cauliflower (Recipes used in: Paleo Fiesta Fish Tacos, Sweetened Cauliflower Rice), Frozen Beets (Recipes used in: Beet and Berry Smoothie, Beet, Carrot and Yam Soup)

Vital Proteins: Collagen Peptides (Recipes used in: Sweet Potato Crepes, Straight From the Tropics Green Chia Seed Pudding, Matcha Raisin Overnight Oats, Peppermint Mocha Caffeine Free Overnight Oats, Chocoberry Green Smoothie, Antioxidant Booster Smoothie)

PRODUCT WEBSITES

Thrive Market: http://www.thrivemarket.com

Amazon: http://www.amazon.com.

Whole Foods Market: http://www.wholefoodsmarket.com.

Search Wellness: http://www.searchwellness.com. (For Beet Root Powder)

REFERENCES

Daniels, N. Berry Boosters: *Acai, Macqui, and Many Other Popular Berries That Will Change Your Life and Health.* BookRix, 2013.

Ezz El-Arab AM, Girgis SM, Hegazy EM, Abd El-Khalek AB. "Effect of dietary honey on intestinal microflora and toxicity of mycotoxins in mice," *BMC Complement Altern Med.* 2006;6:6. https://www.ncbi.nlm.nih.gov/pmc/articles/PMC1431562/. Published March 14, 2006.

Hutt, A. "What is a Functional Food?" The Institute of Food Technologists website. http://www.ift.org/Knowledge-Center/Learn-About-Food-Science/Food-Facts/What-is-a-functional-food.aspx. Published February 2, 2016. Accessed October 27, 2019.

Katz, R., Edeleson, M. *The Longevity Kitchen.* Ten Speed Press. Berkeley, CA. 2013.

Mills, S., Bone, K. *Principles and Practice of Phytotherapy.* Churchill Livingstone. London. 2000.

Newman, F., Lankskey, E. *Pomegranate: The Most Medicinal Fruit.* Basic Health Publications, Inc. Laguna Beach, CA. 2007.

Parsnip. Raw Food Guru Website. https://rawfood.guru/parsnip/. September 10, 2019.

Pitchford, P. *Healing with Whole Foods.* North Atlantic Books. Berkeley, CA. 1993.

Reinhard, T. *Super Foods: The Healthiest Foods on The Planet.* Firefly Books. Buffalo, NY. 2014.

Stefanson, AL, Bakovic, M. "Falcarinol Is a Potent Inducer of Heme Oxygenase-1 and Was More Effective than Sulforaphane in Attenuating Intestinal Inflammation at Diet-Achievable Levels." *Oxidative Medicine and Cell Longevity*. 2018. Abstract retrieved from https://www.ncbi.nlm.nih.gov/pubmed/30420908.

Sorghum. Grains and Legumes Nutrition Counsel Website. https://www.glnc.org.au/grains/types-of-grains/sorghum/. 2019.

CPSIA information can be obtained
at www.ICGtesting.com
Printed in the USA
LVHW060531220720
661203LV00006B/585